D0075119

GREAT BOOKS

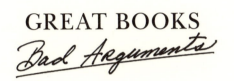
Bad Arguments

GREAT BOOKS

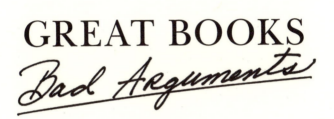
Bad Arguments

Republic, Leviathan,
&
The Communist Manifesto

W. G. RUNCIMAN

PRINCETON UNIVERSITY PRESS
PRINCETON AND OXFORD

Published by Princeton University Press, 41 William Street, Princeton,
New Jersey 08540

In the United Kingdom: Princeton University Press, 6 Oxford Street,
Woodstock, Oxfordshire OX20 1TW

Library of Congress Cataloging-in-Publication Data

Runciman, W. G. (Walter Garrison), 1934–
Great books, bad arguments : Republic, Leviathan, and The Communist
Manifesto / W. G. Runciman.
        p.   cm.
Includes bibliographical references.
ISBN 978-0-691-14476-4 (cloth : alk. paper)
1. Political science—Philosophy. 2. Plato. Republic. 3. Hobbes,
Thomas, 1588–1679. Leviathan. 4. Marx, Karl, 1818–1883. Manifest der
Kommunistischen Partei. English. I. Title.
        JA71.R68 2010
        320.01—dc22   2009039248

British Library Cataloging-in-Publication Data is available

This book has been composed in Bembo

Printed on acid-free paper. ∞

press.princeton.edu

Printed in the United States of America

3 5 7 9 10 8 6 4 2

CONTENTS

PREFACE

This book is intended, as its title suggests, to be provocative. But there is nothing unserious about the purpose behind it. Different readers may have different answers from mine to the question which prompted me to write it. But I hope that all will agree that the question is one which deserves to be asked.

I have been deliberately sparing in the references I have given to such of the extensive secondary literature as I have consulted. This is partly because, to borrow some words of Hobbes's, "Commentaries are more commonly subject to cavill than the text; and therefore need other Commentaries; and so there will be no end of such Interpretation." But it is also because I would like readers, whether less or more familiar with these texts than myself, to go back to them directly in order to make up their minds whether they agree with me or not. If there is somewhere a commentary on one or other of the texts which, if I knew of it, would compel me to retract one or more comments of my own, I would be grateful to have it brought to my notice.

All quotations are from the following editions: *Republic* = *Platonis Res Publica*, edited by J. Burnet (Oxford 1902); *Leviathan* = Thomas Hobbes, *Leviathan*, revised student edition, edited by R. Tuck (Cambridge 1996); *The Communist Manifesto* = *Manifest der Kommunistischen Partei* in *Marx/Engels Gesamtausgabe*, Band 6 (Berlin 1932). Translations from *Republic* and *The Communist Manifesto* are my own.

My thanks are due to Hilary Edwards for the preparation of the manuscript for publication, to Ian Malcolm for its acceptance by Princeton University Press, and to the Council of Trinity College, Cambridge, for its continuing support.

March 2009

GREAT BOOKS
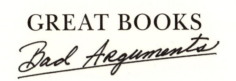

Chapter One

INTRODUCTION

1

Some years ago, I had a conversation with the philosopher Myles Burnyeat in which I asked him how a book like Plato's *Republic* can continue to be admired as it is although so many of the arguments on which it rests are such bad ones. His answer was that I was missing the point: Plato's influence is due to his deliberately not pretending to offer definitive solutions to the questions of enduring interest about which he wishes his readers to reflect. As he subsequently put it in a "Master-Mind" lecture on Plato given at the British Academy, the one thing Plato's commentators ought not to do is pass judgement on his writings as if they were school-room exercises ("Plato, you get four out of ten. Try to do better next time").[1] But why not? *Republic* contains a mixture—some might say a farrago—of arguments of

---

[1] Myles Burnyeat, "Plato," *Proceedings of the British Academy* 111 (2000), p. 7.

different and often puzzling kinds. But if Plato is serious, which he surely is, he wants to persuade his readers that certain propositions in which he firmly believes are true. For the purpose, he deploys a wide range of analogies, similes, metaphors, and myths. But however much more readable these make the book, they have failed in their purpose if the propositions they purport to endorse are at best implausible and at worst demonstrably false.

One possible rejoinder is to insist, with Burnyeat, that all philosophers lend themselves to a diversity of conflicting interpretations and that this is exactly what makes Plato so good to think with. But that won't quite do. *Republic* is not only a work of philosophy. Plato does expound in it metaphysical and epistemological doctrines which, despite all the criticisms to which they have been subjected from Aristotle onwards, are widely regarded as having set much of the agenda for the subsequent practice of philosophy in the European tradition. But it is also a work of sociology. The conclusions to which it invites assent are critically dependent on a set of related propositions about social institutions—that is, about how human beings do, or might, or would behave towards one another under specified historical and environmental conditions. Admittedly, there is no way of conclusively testing speculations about possible states of societies of different kinds until those conditions are realized. But some such speculations are much more solidly grounded than others in what there is good reason to believe to be generally true about how societies function and evolve. To the extent that *Republic* is a work of sociology as well as philosophy, it cannot be exempted from being assessed as such.

It was with that thought in mind that I took down from my shelves the battered copy in which I had first encountered *Republic* as a schoolboy. There I rediscovered the indignant marginal scribbles in which I had protested at arguments which had struck me as not merely feeble but silly, like the perhaps unserious claim that dogs who distinguish friends from foes are philosophers too (376a) and the apparently serious calculation that a tyrant is 729 times more wretched (*anairoteros*) than a philosopher (587e). I found the famous simile of the Cave in book 7, in which the philosopher emerges from a world of shadows into the sunlight, as arresting as ever but the Theory of Forms no more persuasive than before. I was struck all over again by the weakness of Plato's analogy between the "just" (as *dikaios* is conventionally translated) society (*polis*) and the "just" personality (*psychē*) and confirmed in my view by what I found in the secondary literature in which it has since then been analyzed in exhaustive detail. I felt as resistant as ever to Plato's determination to banish poetry and the visual arts from his ideal society. I found his sociology inept, his psychology rudimentary, and his eugenics ridiculous. By the end of book 9, I wondered whether he himself thought his ideal society anything more than an exercise in fantasy, and by the end of book 10, where he falls back for a second time on the prospect of reward in the life to come as the reason for behaving justly in this one (613a; cf. 498c), I wondered how he could fail to realize that he was—to use a present-day metaphor—scoring a spectacular own goal.

At that point, however, I was reminded of what Hobbes says about *Republic* in chapter 31 of *Leviathan*, where he describes himself as being "at the point of believing this my labour, as uselesse, as the Commonwealth of *Plato*" (p. 254). As with *Republic*, I had not reopened my copy of *Leviathan* for over half a century. I remembered it, as I suspect is true of most of its student readers, principally for Hobbes's insistence on the need for power to be concentrated exclusively in the hands of a single Sovereign if a society is not to fall prey to the seditious designs of misguided and unruly subjects. But I was now struck by how Hobbes, after citing *Republic*, voices the hope that "one time or another" his book may fall into the hands of a Sovereign who might "by the exercise of entire Sovereignty, in protecting the Publique teaching of it, convert this Truth of Speculation into the Utility of Practice," just as Plato affirms the hope that even though his ideal society may be, for the moment, a "paradigm laid in heaven" (592b), it might somewhere be realized by someone with the eyes to see it and the power to implement it. Both Plato and Hobbes are not only passionately concerned to find a way for human societies to avoid destructive internal conflict but passionately convinced that the right combination of social practices, roles, and institutions could make it possible. Like *Republic*, *Leviathan* contains a multitude of arguments on a wide range of topics of continuing philosophical interest. But, like *Republic*, it is also a work of sociology which must in the same way be assessed as such. Nobody could plausibly charge Hobbes with simple-mindedness. But many of his commentators have charged him with defending his views about the nature and exercise of power with arguments which are far from being as good as they need to be if his conclusions are to carry conviction. Hobbes's sociology is neither as categorically individualist nor as crudely authoritarian as it has sometimes been represented as being. But the proposition that "whatsoever" a Sovereign once instituted does, "it can be no injury to any of his subjects" (p. 124) is (to put it mildly) not easy to uphold; and no commentator has succeeded in extricating Hobbes from the criticism that, as Bertrand Russell put it in 1946, although he is "the first really modern writer on political theory," he "does not realize the importance of the clash between different classes."[2] He acknowledges the universal desire for assurance of the "power and means to live well" which can never be satisfied "without the acquisition of more" (p. 70). He recognizes that labour

[2] Bertrand Russell, *A History of Western Philosophy* (London, 1946), p. 578.

is "a commodity exchangeable for benefit" (p. 171). He knows that Sovereigns have to extract surplus resources from their subjects by way of taxation if they are to fulfil their function of preserving the internal peace of the Commonwealth and protecting it from its external enemies. But he fails to anticipate that what he calls "Leagues of Subjects" acting in their economic, rather than their political, roles might be as much of a threat to the stability of the Commonwealth as the overtly political Factions which conspire to take the Sword out of the Sovereign's hands into their own. As the quotation from Russell shows, it is not only Marxists who have concluded that Hobbes's analysis of the causes of "civil warre" is flawed for that if no other reason. How can a book which is, according to Richard Tuck, "generally held to be the masterpiece of English political thought" (p. ix) be held to be so when it ignores as it does the sociological significance of conflicts of economic, as opposed to ideological or political, power?

But then I reflected that this rhetorical question might be a reflection of a judgement too much influenced in hindsight by Marx. For Marxist historians, England's Great Rebellion was not a struggle between rival ideological communities or political factions so much as a defining event in England's evolution out of a feudal mode of production into a capitalist mode through the revolutionary transfer of economic power into the hands of the bourgeoisie. But is Hobbes to be faulted for not having seen it as such? That further question sent me, once I had finished rereading *Leviathan*, back to *The Communist Manifesto*, which I now reread in the original German text as printed in London in February of 1848. When I did so, it provoked much the same reaction as rereading *Republic* and *Leviathan* had done. *The Communist Manifesto* is very much what it says it is: a manifesto. It is not a treatise so much as a call to arms. But no less than either *Republic* or *Leviathan*, it asks its readers to accept a set of sociological propositions which, if they cannot be upheld, must lead to acceptance being withheld; and they cannot be upheld. So, once again: how can so admired a text be based on such bad arguments?

2

In the chapters to follow, I address only those passages in the three books which bear on their concern with the design of some set arrangements by which harmony and order could be achieved and sustained in human societies. All three take as their starting point a state of the world in which power is unequally shared between those who rule and those who are ruled—in *Republic*, the "*archontes*" and the "*archoumenoi*"; in *Leviathan*, the "Soveraigne Power" and the "Subjects"; in *The Communist Manifesto*, the "*Unterdrücker*" and the "*Unterdrückte*." Among the various institutional forms which this relationship takes, some may be more willingly accepted

than others by the ruled, and some may be more fre-
quently disrupted by more or less violent protests. No
society can be completely free of conflict and dissent,
and all contain some individuals who behave in ways
which violate the norms by which, in their society,
criminality is culturally defined. But Plato, Hobbes, and
Marx have all set themselves to propose a form of government which, once brought into effect, would bring
to an end the conflicts which pit different groups or
combinations of the ruled against the rulers, or each
other, or both, in attempts either to alter the distribution of power in their favour or to subvert the existing
system of its distribution entirely.

This way of putting it may invite objection from historians and philosophers of history who, in the spirit of
Collingwood, want to insist that the three texts cannot
be properly understood, let alone compared with one
another, unless they are interpreted in recognition of the
very different historical and political circumstances under which they were written. Collingwood himself put
the point directly in his *Autobiography*, when he asked
whether *Republic* and *Leviathan*, so far as they are concerned with politics, could be said to "represent two
different theories of the same thing."[3] His answer was a
categorical no, because the "state about which Plato is
writing is the Greek *polis* and Hobbes's is the absolutist

[3]R. G. Collingwood, *An Autobiography* (Oxford, 1939), p. 67.

state of the seventeenth century." But the objection rests on a pre-emptive assumption about what is meant by "the same thing." Nobody denies the magnitude of the cultural and social differences between the Athens of Pericles and the England of Charles I: as Collingwood put it, "the thing has got *diablement changé en route*." But it does not follow that the same questions cannot be asked and answered about the practices, roles, and institutions of the two societies and comparisons drawn between them by reference to the answers given. There could be no such thing as a "theory of the state" if there had to be as many theories as there are states, or if questions about their different methods of selection for political office, or taxation, or military conscription, or passing or amending or annulling legislation could not be answered except in terms with meanings unique to each. To those who allege that comparative sociology cannot be done, the best rejoinder is not to engage in philosophical argument with Collingwood about the "logical bluff" of which he accuses his "realist" opponents but simply to do it; and to those who allege that Plato's, Hobbes's, and Marx's different answers to the question "Can internal social conflict be prevented?" are answers to different questions, the best rejoinder is to look at their answers and then compare them. If their different answers are then judged to have failed for different reasons, that does not mean that they are not failures in pursuit of the same common aim.

From the perspective of comparative sociology, their respective answers to the question which concerns them all turn out to be categorically different in the relative priority they assign to the three forms of power—political, ideological, and economic—by which the incumbents of institutional roles in any and all societies dominate, or are dominated by, each other. Admittedly, none of them conceptualized the roles constitutive of the societies they were writing about as vectors in a three-dimensional social space or estimated rates and distances of inter- and intra-generational social mobility of individuals between higher- and lower-ranked roles in the way that a present-day sociologist might do. But whatever the different idioms in which they do it, all three are talking about how the strong exercise their power over the weak. For Marx, there is no doubt that it is control of the means of production which is the overriding determinant of the distribution of power.[4] In contrast, both Plato and Hobbes, for different reasons of their own, underestimate the importance of both the forces and the social relations of production. But whereas for Hobbes, despite his recognition of the need

---

[4]Even if that is not unequivocally stated anywhere in *The Communist Manifesto*, it is so stated in *Capital* (vol. 3, p. 791 in the Moscow English-language edition of 1966), where it is said that "It is *always* [my italics] the direct relationship of the owners of the conditions of production to the direct producers ... which reveals the innermost secret, the hidden basis of the entire social structure, and with it the political form of the relation of sovereignty and dependence, in short, the corresponding specific form of the state."

for the Sovereign to use his control of the means of persuasion to best advantage, it is the Sovereign's control of the means of coercion which is decisive, for Plato, despite his recognition of the need for the Guardians to deploy their and their Auxiliaries' control of the means of coercion to best advantage, it is control of the means of persuasion on which he relies to keep the lower orders in their place. This difference is critical to both the strengths and the weaknesses of their respective attempts to set out how rulers must behave if they are to be accorded legitimacy by the ruled and use it to preserve internal peace. But none of their attempts succeeds, whichever the form of power held to override, if not determine, the other two.

A different possible objection to the task I have set myself is that sociology is not a branch of academic enquiry sufficiently advanced for judgements of success or failure to be as authoritatively pronounced as I appear to think possible. Some readers, indeed, may be as dismissive of sociologists as Plato was of the "Sophists" of whom he so strongly disapproved, as Hobbes was of the "philosophy schools" whose teachings he ridiculed, and as Marx was of the "petty-bourgeois" socialists whose theories he regarded as at the same time utopian and reactionary. But in the course of the last hundred years, there have been not only many important and well-validated discoveries made in the specialized sciences of human behaviour but also many important and well-validated additions made to the evidence accumulated in the historical, ethnographic, and archaeological record about the workings of human societies of different kinds. It may not be possible to correct—to mark out of ten, if you like—Plato's or Hobbes's or Marx's sociology in the way that could be done for their biology or their physics. But it is entirely possible to point out the limits of their understanding of the range of different ways in which, in societies of different kinds, shared beliefs, representations, and norms relate to economic, ideological, and political institutions and these relate to one another. On three topics in particular, Plato, Hobbes, and Marx can alike be faulted not only for mistakes which they make about the causes of internal conflict but for their neglect of mechanisms and processes whose capacity to reduce and contain it they fail to consider at all.

First, all three underestimate the contribution which the institutional separation of powers can make to the preservation of internal peace. It is not only Hobbes who sees any sharing of power as an inevitable diminution of the Sovereign's capacity to keep order among the ruled. Plato's requirement that in a just society the members of each of his three categories must, unless individually promoted or demoted from one category to another, perform only their own appointed function betrays his fear that if the Philosopher-Kings and their Auxiliaries do not retain an exclusive monopoly of power, the society will start to fall apart. In the case of

The Communist Manifesto, Marx and Engels make what is in effect the same point when they say in their preface to the German edition of 1872 that the experience of the Paris Commune has proved that the proletariat cannot wield the existing machinery of the bourgeois state for its own purposes but must abolish and replace it. The idea that social stability might be sustained by ongoing intermediate institutions whose autonomous power might be deployed in the service of successive rulers is as alien to the thought of Plato, Hobbes, and Marx as it is intrinsic to that of Montesquieu, Tocqueville, and Durkheim.

Second, all three underestimate the scope for collaboration between the members of different systacts—whether these are orders, classes, status groups, castes, age sets, or any other sets of similarly located roles—who, even if competitors for power, have a common interest in sustaining the institutions within which their rivalry is acted out. Plato believes that the Producers—the artisans, farmers, and businessmen whom he ranks together—will curb their appetites and defer as they should to their superiors only because they have been persuaded that their superiors are better men than they. Hobbes, while well aware of the mutual cooperation which binds together individuals engaged in criminal or conspiratorial activities, believes that only the fear of physical coercion can lead them to cooperate as they should with the Sovereign and the Sovereign's agents.

Marx, while recognizing that cooperation between proletarians is critical to the overthrow of the bourgeois
state, believes that cooperation between proletariat and
bourgeoisie can only arise where engineered through
bribery, deception, or fraud. But active and willing cooperation across systactic boundaries is commonplace in
human societies in the economic, ideological, and political dimensions of power alike.

Third, all three underestimate the extent to which
both cultural and social evolution come about through a
process, not of either one-way progress in the direction
of unanimity and peace or one-way regression in the direction of chaos and strife, but of continuous variation,
competition, and trade-off. Mutations in cultural representations and social practices succeed or fail according
to the environmental conditions which either enhance
or diminish their probability of reproduction and diffusion in the populations carrying them. For Plato, order depends on the ability of the Guardians to maintain
their hold over the minds of the ruled. For Hobbes, it
depends on the ability of the Sovereign to exact continuing and virtually unconditional obedience from the
ruled. For Marx, it depends on the ability of the vic-
torious proletariat to do away with the exploitation of
the ruled by the rulers which has been the source of
class conflict hitherto. But in all societies, existing representations, beliefs, and attitudes are continually being
reformulated at the same time that existing economic,

ideological, and political practices are continually being renegotiated. The maintenance of harmony and order depends, not on an optimal institutional design which, if it can once be realized, will remain in place for the indefinite future, but on an adaptive and flexible mixture of practices capable of moderating and containing both inter-personal and inter-systactic conflict.

More generally still, all three share a common reluctance to meet head-on the challenge which Plato puts into the mouth of the rhetorician Thrasymachus in the opening book of *Republic*. Plato makes Thrasymachus say, in a deliberately crude and offensive tirade, that "injustice" is in every way better than "justice," which is in any case nothing other than what the strong impose on the weak. But his rejection of Socrates' claim that justice is both intrinsically good and inherently beneficial to those who practise it demands a much more effective rejoinder than Socrates gives it. Thrasymachus is the prototype of the saloon-bar realist who knows that life is a jungle in which people all lie and cheat whenever they see it as in their interest to do so provided that they can escape getting caught. Nice guys finish last, suckers don't deserve an even break, politicians are in it for themselves, and morality is for the birds. Plato, Hobbes, and Marx are all convinced in their different ways that once the right people are in power, they will want to do the right thing and will know how to do it, so that harmony and order will thereafter prevail.

But, says Thrasymachus, just look around you! Anyone not distracted by specious philosophical chit-chat from seeing the world as it is knows that the people who will always come off best are those most determined to pursue their own interests at the expense of everyone else. Plato supposes that his Philosopher-Kings will devote themselves unstintingly to the good of society as a whole. Hobbes supposes that his Sovereigns will follow the God-given Laws of Nature in the exercise of their Sovereignty. Marx supposes that his proletarians will use their seizure of power from the bourgeoisie in order to put an end to any possibility of conflict between exploiters and exploited. But, says Thrasymachus, it is pure naivety—he explicitly addresses Socrates as "o most naïve" (*ō euēthestate*) at 343d2—not to expect those who have power to extend it as far as they can. Indeed, the further they do, the more they will be admired for it, conquerors most of all. His challenge, even when less extravagantly stated than Plato makes it, is not unanswerable. But how effectively does Plato answer it? Or Hobbes? Or Marx?

Chapter Two

REPUBLIC

1

Gilbert Ryle, in the review that he published in 1947 of Karl Popper's *The Open Society and Its Enemies*, stated the prosecution case against the arguments of *Republic* as forcibly as anyone, including Popper himself: "No tutor would accept from a pupil the reasons given by Plato for the following quite important doctrines: that the Soul is tri-partite; that if the Soul is tri-partite, the ideal society would be a three-class state; that whatever exists, exists to perform one and only one function; that reason is one such function; that one and only one of the classes should be taught to reason; that membership of a class should normally be determined by pedigree; that empirical science can never be 'real' science; that there are Forms; that only knowledge of Forms is 'real science'; that only those who have this knowledge can have good political judgement; that political institutions must degenerate unless there are rulers who have had the sort of education that Plato describes; that 'justice' consists in doing one's own job; and so on." Ryle does not then offer any counter-argument on Plato's behalf or even hint that he might himself be exaggerating the strength of the prosecution case. Instead, he goes on to say that *Republic* "is not primarily an enquiry. It is a sermon—if it is not a manifesto (or is it, perhaps, more than anything else, an attempt to explain to the uneducated the purposes of the curriculum of the higher education which Plato was in process of providing?)."[1]

But a sermon, no less than an enquiry, is vulnerable to criticism of the quality of the arguments from which its injunctions and prescriptions are derived. So is a manifesto, as chapter 4 will further illustrate. Plato may have chosen to deploy what he knew to be some questionable rhetorical devices in order to make more palatable to his readers conclusions which he wished them to accept. Since he envisages the Guardians of his ideal society persuading their inferiors to see that they belong where they are by teaching them myths which the Guardians themselves know to be untrue (414b–c), why should he scruple to treat the readers of *Republic* in the same way? But *pace* Ryle, his audience was not the uneducated, any more than it is now. He was not addressing the rude mechanicals and clod-hopping rustics of Athens and the Attic countryside but those of his fellow

---

[1]Gilbert Ryle, review of Popper, *Mind* 56 (1947): 170.

gentry whose intellectual interests were the same as his own. An important part of his sermon is indeed directed to the desirability of a thorough training in philosophy for those capable of practising it. But that is with a view to placing such people in positions of power after they have returned, in the famous metaphor, from the sunlight into the cave where their ignorant fellow citizens are still living in the world of shadows, which is all that they know. The sermon (if such it is) is being preached to an audience presumed fully capable of understanding his arguments in favour of the kind of society that a Philosopher-King would bring into being; and if, when scrutinized, that society is constituted by a set of institutions which is impracticable to the point of impossibility, the higher education curriculum loses its political relevance altogether.

There is nothing inherently misconceived in the idea that in a just society—whatever "just" turns out to mean—the rulers should be those of its citizens best qualified to make and keep it so. But what does this mean in practice? Plato's analogies of the diligent shepherd, the well-trained doctor, and the clear-eyed steersman have been criticised time and again for begging the question of what is the end towards which their exercise of their skills is directed. He puts into the mouth of Thrasymachus (343b) the pertinent observation that herdsmen look after their herds in order to benefit themselves, not the beasts they tend, but Socrates nowhere answers it as it requires: he merely asserts (345d) that shepherding is about nothing other than making the best possible provision for what it is set in charge of (*eph'hō tetaktai*). Nor does Socrates resolve the difficulty that there are no agreed criteria by which to measure the health of a human society as there are to measure that of a human body, any more than there is an equivalent for the "ship of state" of the agreed destination to which the steersman is conveying the passengers on board. Although it is true that there are mental illnesses just as there are bodily ones, Plato equates mental health with the state of mind which informs and motivates behaviour of the kind of which he personally approves. It is entirely plausible to assume that a society will not be harmonious or orderly if its rulers are stupid and cowardly. Nor is there anything inherently misconceived in the analogy between a disciplined society and a disciplined person: a disciplined society is one whose potentially disruptive members its rulers have under control, and a disciplined person is one whose reason has under control the passions and appetites which might otherwise break out in antisocial behaviour. The trouble, however, lies in Plato's insistence that the three distinct parts of the *psychē* (the rational, the passionate, and the appetitive) correspond to the three distinct parts which (slaves and women apart) make up his *polis*—the Guardians (who are rational), the Auxiliaries (who are passionate), and the artisans, farmers, and businessmen (who are appetitive).

I have remarked already on the extent of the philosophical literature in which the *polis/psychē* analogy has been dissected in detail. Self-defeating for Plato's depiction of his ideal society as his recourse to it may be, the arguments by which he supports it are sufficiently ingenious that the reasons for which they fail are well worth the attention which philosophers have accorded them. But from a sociological point of view, the critical question is how far the predicated attributes of societies of the different kinds which Plato distinguishes from one another are a function of the attributes of their members. In book 4, Socrates is made to say that a *polis* must share the "forms and characters" (*eidē* and *ēthē*) of its citizens (435e), which has landed Plato in almost as much trouble from the commentators as the tripartite division of both *polis* and *psychē*. There is nothing odd in saying, for example, that a warlike society is a society of warlike people, as opposed to saying, for example, that a large society is a society of large people. Nor does Plato's Socrates ever say anything as foolish as that. But in book 8, where he sets out his taxonomy of unjust societies and their distinguishing characteristics, he apparently fails to see the difference between saying that the citizens of what he calls a "timocratic" society are mostly, if not all, timocratic—that is, motivated by the desire for personal prestige—and saying that the citizens of a "tyrannical" society are mostly, if not all, tyrannical. No doubt the tyrant is a tyrannically minded person, and an enquiring sociologist might well find that the henchmen on whom the tyrant relies to keep his subjects obedient to his wishes are tyrannically minded too. But the tyrannized, as the commentators have not been slow to point out, are not themselves tyrannical, and Plato himself acknowledges it when he says of the tyrannized *polis* that the free men who constitute the best element within it are reduced to a dishonourable and miserable servitude (577c). Whether a just society could be created and sustained by being predominantly, even if not exclusively, populated by just citizens therefore depends on what is meant by justice as manifested in the behaviour of the rulers towards the ruled. If a just man is just in the same way (441d) as a *polis* is just, this might mean not that a just *polis* is full of just people but that it is one in which the just minority has the unjust majority under control in the way that a just man has under control his temptations to behave unjustly. Which is it? The answer, as Bernard Williams has shown, is that the use of the analogy is to help Plato to have it both ways.[2]

Plato is well aware that his conception of justice departs from normal usage. As is made clear in the conversation with which the dialogue opens in the house of a financially successful and conventionally minded resident alien, the standard meaning of "the just thing"

---

[2]Bernard Williams, "The Analogy of City and Soul in Plato's *Republic*," in *The Sense of the Past* (Princeton, 2006), p. 111. (First published in 1973.)

(*to dikaion*) is that it consists in giving everyone their due. The *dikaios* man pays his taxes, performs his civic and religious duties, repays his obligations, keeps his promises, and goes to his grave in self-satisfied awareness that he has made his money without cheating. Kenneth Dover, in his authoritative study of popular morality in Plato's time, says that "Honest administration of money or property entrusted to one's safe-keeping is normally treated as a manifestation—almost the manifestation *par excellence*—of *dikaiosynē*."[3] Plato, however, is looking for more than this at both the social and the personal level. His just society is not merely one in which the constitution is impartially administered, taxes are spent for the general good, contracts are upheld by the courts, citizens perform their public duties as and when required, and anyone who steals another's property or assaults another by violence is caught and punished. It is also a society in which the members of every category of citizen perform only the functions appropriate to that category. The just man is not merely one who gives everyone his due but one who subordinates his personal interests and preferences to the well-being of the society of which he is a member by unquestioningly accepting his station and his duties within it: *dikaiosynē*, Socrates tells Glaucon (433a–b) is "to do one's own things" (*ta*

[3] K. J. Dover, *Greek Popular Morality in the Time of Plato and Aristotle* (Oxford, 1974), p. 44.

hautou prattein). Some commentators are understandably unhappy about "just" as the generally accepted English translation of *dikaios*, and in some passages "righteous" captures the appropriate nuance more closely. But whatever the right word, or words, in which to render it in English, Socrates goes on to specify in some detail the substantive conditions that "just" persons and societies must fulfil if they are to come as close as possible to the Form of the Good. The mistake which he then makes, irrespective of how far he is committed to the proposition that most, if not all, of the citizens of a just society must themselves be just, is to suppose that a society which meets his conditions is bound to be more harmonious and orderly than one which does not, and a person who meets them less troubled by a conflict of motives than one who either can't or doesn't want to meet them.

The idea that in a harmonious and orderly society the citizens will perform the tasks for which they are best suited may, at first sight, seem as unobjectionable as the idea that rulers should be properly qualified to rule. When Socrates, in book 2, considers what it is that brings a society into being in the first place, he points to the division of labour which is dictated by mutual need: the farmer will farm the land, the builder will build the houses, the weaver will weave the clothes, the shoemaker will make the shoes, and they will exchange the products of their labour to their acknowledged mutual benefit. He then allows that, as Glaucon is made to remind him, human societies do not remain in the simple state that he has initially depicted but have to confront the problems which arise from the emergence of a wider range of occupational roles, the enlargement of the society's territory, the growth of trade, and the threat of foreign invasion. This evolution is depicted in moralistic terms which betray Plato's unrelenting disapproval not only of moneymakers but of practitioners of the mimetic arts. But sociologically, there is nothing wrong with it if we substitute for Plato's farmer, builder, weaver, and shoemaker the members of the hunting and foraging bands which historically preceded the settled communities in which growing population, accumulation of surplus resources, and increasing density of occupation of territory generated a hitherto nonexistent requirement for institutionalized social control. Plato, however, goes on to insist on the necessity for a just society to enforce a division of function between his three separate systacts of Guardians, Auxiliaries, and Producers so strict that if a shoemaker wishes to move out of his role as shoemaker he must be compelled to remain in it (374b). Later, Socrates concedes that it won't matter too much if a shoemaker wants to try his hand at building, or a builder at shoemaking (434a). But for a Producer to try to become an Auxiliary, or an Auxiliary a Guardian, is *polypragmosynē*—the urge to meddle in others' business, which Socrates goes so far as to denounce (434c) as "exceptional wickedness" (*malista kakourgia*). This, un-surprisingly, has upset liberal-minded commentators for whom the denial of freedom to move out of one social role into another except under compulsion is an example of blatant *in*justice. But there is nothing unworkable about it. In Late Imperial Rome, Hindu India, and Tsarist Russia, for example, rulers have put into place effective institutional sanctions by which workers have been compelled to follow their fathers' occupations and remain in them for life. Plato's difficulty is that he wants the members of the two subordinate systacts to agree that this restriction of their freedom is for their own good as well as the rulers'. They are not subjected to the sort of direct coercive control which they themselves exercise over the slaves who are, to the surprise of some commentators, still there in the just society (433d). But they do not need to be, since they have been educated by the rulers to be reconciled to their designated roles.

All rulers, no doubt, would like those whom they rule to be content with their lot, however little they may scruple to use force to maintain themselves in power if threatened by rebellion. But the history of attempts to bring about that state of affairs through the exercise of monopoly control of the means of persuasion is a history of almost total failure. The ruled may not overtly challenge the ideology imposed on them by the rulers and may even be unaware of possible alternatives. But ideological conformity is no guarantee of political stability. The subjects of a Christian king may have been exposed to no other teachings than those of a Church which enjoins obedience and brotherly love, but the history of Christianity discloses the perennial ineffectiveness of clerical appeals, injunctions, and threats. The subjects of a "rightly guided" Islamic caliph may never have questioned the authority of the Quran, but the history of Islam is full of violent sectarian conflict both within and between Islamic societies. The subjects of a hegemonic Communist Party may have been inculcated from childhood with the precepts of Marxism-Leninism, but the history of Communism illustrates just how little purpose-built rituals and symbols can do to remould the temperament and character of a people. No amount of indoctrination, even from an early age, is ever so effective that no independent-minded nonconformists ever question the representations, beliefs, and attitudes handed down by rulers and their auxiliary propagandists, professors, and priests.

When it comes to the psychological state of the individual citizen, Plato is on safe ground in emphasizing the extent to which motives can conflict. Indeed, he might think his picture of the *psychē* as composed of separate parts amply vindicated by present-day brain science, which makes it possible to observe directly what is happening in different parts of the brain as ratiocination and emotion respectively come into play. But he is wedded to a preconceived and empirically unsustainable belief that psychic harmony—or, as we might say, a well-adjusted personality—is attainable only by someone who is steadfastly and consistently disposed to behave in ways which, by his criteria, count as just. This invites the immediate rejoinder that not only are there unjust people among both rulers and ruled who are entirely at ease with themselves and untroubled by conflicts of motive, but there are also just people whose wish to further the interests of their society as they perceive them presents them with dilemmas which trouble their peace of mind both before and after they have decided which of a number of possible courses of action to pursue. For Plato, the unjust man is guilty by definition of *pleonexia*—the excessive desire for more than he has. The man dominated by reason is not pleonectic, since his desire is for as close an acquaintance with the Form of the Good as it is possible to attain, whereas the man dominated by passion is pleonectic in his desire for honour and victory and the man dominated by appetite is pleonectic in his desire for money and the pleasures of the flesh. But why cannot a "timocratic" man be satisfied with a moderate amount of honour, or a "chrematistic" man with a moderate amount of money? From the viewpoint of moral philosophy, Plato may have good reasons for disapproving of people who prefer the pursuit of honour or money to the pursuit of knowledge, and disapproving of them still more if they display not only indifference to philosophy but contempt for those who practise it—even if, as Socrates agrees with Adeimantus in book 6, many philosophers are charlatans (487d). But he has no good reason to refuse to admit the possibility that such people may be no less successful than philosophers in reconciling, to their own peace of mind, the claims of reason, passion, and appetite.

2

The further anomaly in all this is that Socrates' just society, once he has fully described it, entirely fails to provide the refutation of Thrasymachus which Glaucon and Adeimantus have pressed Socrates to give them at the beginning of book 2. Thrasymachus has by then rejected the option offered him by another of the participants in the conversation of defining "justice" as whatever the stronger compel the weaker to do (340b). He has also conceded that it is not true that rulers always exercise their power to their own advantage at the expense of the ruled, since rulers are quite capable of making mistakes and the ruled of combining successfully against them; and although he regards injustice as a virtue, he does not regard justice as a vice but only as naivety (*euētheia*) of a "noble" (*gennaia*) kind (348c). But the arguments by which Plato allows Socrates to extract from him a grudging assent to the propositions that justice is a virtue and injustice a vice, and that the *dikaios* man will live well and the *adikos* one badly (353e), are notoriously inadequate. The recent commentators all agree on their inadequacy: they disagree only about how inadequate they are and how far Plato should be supposed to be aware of it. At the close of book 1, Thrasymachus drops out of the argument on a note of wholly ironic assent to Socrates' triumphant conclusion that *adikia* is never more profitable than *dikaiosynē*, and when he reappears at the beginning of book 5, after Socrates has given his exposition of *dikaiosynē* in society and the individual, it is only to join in encouraging him to enlarge on his startling proposals for the communal sharing (*koinōnia*) of women and children (449c) by the Guardians. But if Plato had allowed him to return to his original theme that what passes as justice is nothing more than the prescriptions imposed on the weak by the strong, he could have put it to Socrates that his ideally just society is an example of precisely that. The Guardians, assisted as necessary by the Auxiliaries, use their power to compel the Producers to conform to what the Guardians choose to call justice—that is, their self-serving, self-chosen principle that every man is to mind nobody's business but his own.

The anomaly is all the more puzzling because Socrates has accepted the challenge put to him by Adeimantus and Glaucon who, although they do not themselves agree with Thrasymachus, want a better argument than Socrates has given Thrasymachus against the claim that injustice is preferable to justice as a way of life. Again, there has been much discussion by the commentators of the implications of their request from the viewpoint of moral philosophy. But whatever those implications may be, the brothers explicitly ask to be shown both why anyone would choose to pursue justice as an aim in itself even when under no compulsion to behave justly and why anyone would choose to do anything more than pretend to be just if there is an equal advantage to be gained by seeming, although not being, so. In book 10, Socrates claims that by the end of his life the *dikaios* man will, like a long-distance runner at the finish of a race (613c), receive his reward at last. But if behaving justly pays off at the end of the day in tangible rewards, the reason to act justly is purely instrumental and the appearance of being an authentically just person will do quite as well as the reality.

Despite the widespread dissatisfaction with Plato's failure to give a more convincing response than he does, no commentator has (so far as I can discover) pointed out the affinity between the brothers' concerns and the concerns of present-day sociologists seeking to find a satisfactory explanation for behaviour which advances the interests of others at an unreciprocated cost to the agent. In the speech in which Thrasymachus pointedly addresses Socrates as "o most naïve," he charges him with being unaware that *dikaiosynē* is an "other-regarding" good (*allotrion agathon*): the *dikaios* man suffers self-inflicted harm (*oikeia blabē*) for the benefit of someone stronger than himself (343c). The *dikaios*, in other words, is an altruist, while the *adikos* is an egoist who will lie, cheat, free-ride, defect, or renege on a promise whenever he will enhance his chances of winning by doing so. He is the supremely rational game theorist. As Adeimantus puts it, he enters a competition (*agōn*) expressly in order to come out on top (*perigignesthai*) and to *pleonektein* at the opponent's expense (362b). He well understands the costing of search time in the quest for altruists to play against,[4] the potential gains from playing mixed or random strategies, and the rationale for forming or joining coalitions. He knows all about the "handicap effect"—that is, he knows when to put himself at an apparent disadvantage in order to convey to his opponent his confidence in his own superiority. He is skilled at fake signalling and will put on the appearance of putting others' interests before his own whenever a reputation for altruism will work to his advantage. He will, of course, defect in one-shot Prisoner's Dilemma but, in a series of games, be ready to play "tit-for-tat" or "win-stay, lose-shift," or whatever alternative strategy will maximize his gains over the longer term. And in an Ultimatum Game, he will behave exactly as the textbooks

---

[4]This point is in effect made, without reference to game theory, by T.Y. Henderson, "In Defense of Thrasymachus," *American Philosophical Quarterly* 7 (1970): 223, when he correctly points out that "the greater the ratio of just to unjust people in a state, the better life can be for the unjust few."

of economic theory predict: if proposer, he will offer the smallest possible amount, and if responder, will accept whatever he is offered. Why, therefore, doesn't everybody behave like that? Why are there any altruists at all?

Present-day approaches to the problem generally begin from the presumption that natural selection must enhance the probability of reproductive success of egoists relative to that of altruists. Where individual members of a population do sacrifice themselves for others' benefit, it is likely to be either because the beneficiary is genetically related to the altruist or because the altruist anticipates receipt of a reciprocal benefit on some future occasion. Neither of these answers, however, can give the brothers the comfort they are looking for. Kin selection favours the onward transmission of the altruist's genes in accordance with what has now passed into the textbooks as Hamilton's Rule, while reciprocal altruism is not properly speaking altruism at all. Yet there are also, in the inheritance of the human species, two innate dispositions which Thrasymachus ignores but which could be cited to good effect against him. The first is the sense of fellow-feeling aroused by the sight of a person in distress which motivates the Good Samaritans.[5] The second

[5] It is a motive which Hobbes explicitly includes in the chapter of *Leviathan* on "the Interiour Beginnings of Voluntary Motions; commonly called the PASSIONS": "*Griefe*, for the Calamity of another, is PITTY; and ariseth from the imagination that the like calamity may befall himselfe; and therefore is also called COMPASSION, and in the phrase of this present time a FELLOW-FEELING" (p. 43).

is the moralistic indignation aroused by shameless ego-
ism which motivates those confronted with it to strong
reciprocity—that is, punishment both of the egoist and of
those unwilling to do the same. It is, accordingly, false to
assert as Thrasymachus does that nobody behaves altruistically except in the expectation of either a subsequent
benefit which will outweigh the cost or a subsequent
reprisal whose cost will outweigh the benefit. There may
be few if any holy fools who allow themselves to be
willingly exploited on every encounter with an unscrupulous egoist. But there are not that many out-and-out
Thrasymacheans whose violent, rapacious, and deceit-
ful pursuit of personal advantage is never tempered by
an occasional display of kindness or acknowledgement
of guilt. Most people behave egoistically at some times
and altruistically at others, and most social institutions
are kept in being by cooperation based on interpersonal
trust as well by formal economic, ideological, and political sanctions. Societies cohere, and internal disorder is
contained, not only through the power of the rulers and
the weakness of the ruled but through the willingness
of the citizens to refrain from taking advantage of each
other on every occasion, even when the rational cost-
benefit strategy would be to do so.

This line of argument is, however, not open to Plato.
He portrays both the rulers and the ruled in his ideal
society as altruists. But they are altruists in a way that
Thrasymachus could plausibly construe as supporting

his case. The rulers are, we are told, philosophers who have consented to abandon the contemplative life for the life of guardianship and the self-sacrificial dedication to the welfare of the whole society which that entails: when, at the beginning of book 4, Adeimantus says that they will enjoy none of what other rulers enjoy in the way of land and fine houses and possession of silver and gold and the means to perform their sacrifices and entertain their friends as they please (419a), Socrates at first replies that the ideal *polis* is not designed to make one *ethnos* within it outstandingly happy, even though he would not be surprised if the Guardians turned out to be as happy as can be (420b). But the life which the Guardians lead is then made to look more and more attractive and their happiness less and less surprising. Their training is arduous and their lifestyle austere. But their material needs are provided for, they are spared the vexation of lawsuits and prosecutions, they have none of the worry of bringing up children, and they are accorded both public privileges in their lifetimes and worthy burials after their deaths (464d–465e). They will even, when sufficiently advanced in age, be allowed to hold political office as they choose and to marry and give in marriage (613d). They are supremely at ease with themselves because they have mastered their passions and appetites and are secure in their consciousness of virtue. But Thrasymachus could respond by saying in his same offensive way that the Guardians are in it for themselves like any other politicians. They have chosen their positions of power, and when they assure those whose lives they control without right of protest or redress that they are subordinating their personal interests to the general good they are simply seeking to strengthen their hold over them. Their pretentions to altruism are nothing more than bullshit.

As for the ruled, they cannot be genuine altruists since they are, in Plato's view, capable only of being trained by their betters to use such capacity for reason as they have to keep their passions and appetites in check. He does at one point envisage the just man with his harmoniously ordered mind preserving the right disposition (*hexis*) whatever activity he is engaged in, whether money-making, looking after his physical well-being, personal affairs, or politics (443e). But the tripartite personalities of the members of the passionate and appetitive systacts are so constituted that it is beyond them to be just in the way that the Guardians are. This comes out in its most *de haut en bas* expression in book 6, where Plato puts into Socrates' mouth an uninhibitedly disdainful portrayal of the banausic aspirants to intellectual status who are compared to a short, bald, recently manumitted tinker who, having made some money, has a bath, puts on new clothes, and sets out to marry his master's impecunious and lonely daughter (495e). Plato's disdain for moneymakers comes out equally uninhibitedly in book 8, where the oligarchic man is depicted as having made both the reasoning and the passionate parts of his personality slaves to his appetite for wealth—and, Socrates assures Adeimantus, is scruffy-looking (*auchmēros*) into the bargain (554a). Thanks to their education and upbringing as arranged for them by the Guardians, the ruled will be willing to further the collective interest of their society as a whole. But this is not the active and self-conscious cooperation of free men motivated by fellow feeling directed towards each other and strong reciprocity directed against Thrasymachean egoists. On the contrary, it is precisely what Thrasymachus had in mind when he said that justice is an "other-regarding good" which works to the advantage of the rulers and a "self-inflicted harm" which works to the disadvantage of the ruled. It is true that the Auxiliaries have been specifically trained not to maltreat (*kakourgein*) their fellow citizens (416d), and Socrates makes clear that he disagrees with Thrasymachus about doing harm (*blabē*) to slaves (590d). But it is the Guardians and Auxiliaries who have the power. The Producers have none. If the Producers are successfully persuaded to acquiesce in their powerlessness by the deception and deceit to which the rulers resort (459c–d), Thrasymachus's response will be: more fools they.

Popper's characterization of a society so organized as "totalitarian," with all the overtones which that word carries in the aftermath of German fascism and Russian communism, has been criticised in its turn as an

overreaction. But as *Republic* progresses, there emerge
more and more details of the workings of Plato's ideal
society which cannot be construed in any way which
does not give support to the substantive content of Popper's indictment. It is not merely that the artisans, farmers, and businessmen must remain in the systact into
which they have been born or to which the Guardians
have assigned them. Even aside from the enforced eugenics and the *koinōnia* of the Guardians' women and
children which Socrates describes to Glaucon (461e) as
"by far the best" arrangement for ensuring the continuing supply of suitable rulers, it is impossible to gloss over
his explicit assertions that when the Philosopher-Kings
come to power, children will be taken away into the
country at the age of ten for indoctrination (541a), and
the mentally unfit (*kata tēn psuchēn kakophueis*) will be
put to death (410a). Nor, when Plato says in the same
sentence that the doctors will allow the sick to die
(*apothnēskein easousin*), does he have in mind voluntary
euthanasia: he means that they will be refused prolonged
medical care. Popper has also been criticised for drawing
an exaggerated contrast between the enlightened egalitarianism which he attributes to the historical Socrates
and the repressive authoritarianism which he attributes
to Plato. But the Socrates of *Republic* expounds a ver-
sion of ostensibly benevolent paternalism which Popper is fully justified in interpreting as no less systematic
a denial of freedom than the kind of tyranny which

Plato represents as being the worst form of government of all. The motivation of Plato's Philosopher-Kings is, of course, very different from that of one of Thrasymachus's conquerors. But the ruled, in his ideal society, are totally dependent for their well-being on the decisions of rulers no more answerable to them than a tyrant would be. No commentator on *Republic*, however attracted to the vision of a *polis* whose rulers are both wise and good, has ever found in it, or ever could, any concession to the idea that a harmonious and orderly society might be more successfully created and maintained by conceding to the ruled a constitutional right of legitimate protest against decisions affecting them in the making of which they have had no say.

3

At the beginning of book 8, Socrates agrees, with Glaucon's encouragement, to go back to the four constitutions (544a) which fall short of the ideal and to rank them in order of good and bad. This, yet again, looks at first sight like a reasonable and straightforward proposal. Why not classify and analyse the current alternatives and by exposing the reasons for their inability to maintain harmony and order bring out all the more clearly the need for the rule of Philosopher-Kings?

But Plato's political sociology turns out to be confused in formulation, illogical in exposition, and implausible in application. The distinction on which he might have been expected to base it is that between monarchy, oligarchy, and democracy—that is, between rule by a single sovereign holding power by either usurpation or inheritance, by a select minority defined by wealth and/or birth, and by an assembly either consisting of or drawn from the general body of citizens (however defined). But instead, Plato lists four types of society which are presented not only as descending in order from good to bad but as succeeding one another in an actual sequence of change. The first is introduced as the widely admired Cretan and Spartan *politeia* (544c), which the reader naturally supposes will then be analyzed by reference to the presumptively harmonious and orderly functioning of contemporary Crete and Sparta. But Socrates instead presents what he calls timocracy as the degenerate form of the aristocracy exemplified by the rule of the Guardians in the just society, and then describes how timocracy degenerates in turn into oligarchy. "Timocratic" societies are dominated by "victory-loving" and "honour-loving" men of the Spartan type (545a) who, in course of time, become money-loving and restrict the occupancy of political offices to the rich (551a–b). Oligarchies then break down because of the intemperate greed of the rich, and the poor, having seized power from them (*nikēsantes*), kill some, banish others, and share political office with the rest (557a). But the seemingly pleasant, anarchic, and variegated democratic *politeia*

(558c) takes freedom to excess, with the result that it provokes a counter-reaction (*eis tounantion metabolē*) and democracy gives rise to tyranny, which is the most extreme and ferocious slavery (*douleia*) of all (564a).

This fable—which is all that it is—has been the despair of commentators who have noticed for a start that Socrates, despite initially conceding that there are other, intermediate constitutions both in Greece and elsewhere, then immediately insists on the necessity (*anangkē*) of equality in the number of types of society and the number of types of men (544d). Any possibility of a coherent reformulation of the fivefold aristocracy/ timocracy/oligarchy/democracy/tyranny typology is therefore ruled out by Plato's refusal to abandon his conviction that the constitution of a society of any given type must reflect the three-tiered psychological makeup of whichever of the three types of citizen is predominant within it. I said earlier that most or all of the citizens of a timocratic society can perfectly well be timocratic in the sense that they are all motivated by a desire for prestige. But Plato has to say that both the timocratic society and the timocratic man are at odds with themselves in the same way; and they obviously aren't. Plato's timocratic man is a person whose passion for prestige has got the better of his reason. But Plato's timocratic society then has to be a society in which pleonectic prestige seekers rule over men whose passions, unlike theirs, are under the control of their reason.

His oligarchic man is similarly conflicted because his passion for money has got the better of his reason. But now Plato's dilemma is that in an oligarchy the rich rule over the poor, but the oligarchs are not men within whom a passionately greedy part controls a rationally ascetic one. In the real world, oligarchies are societies in which power is held by a privileged minority of the citizens who rule over a relatively underprivileged majority, and although the minority may consist predominantly of rich and greedy men and the minority of poor and ascetic ones, it is perfectly possible for the rulers to be ascetic and the ruled greedy—as, come to that, they are in Plato's ideal society. In a democracy, Plato sees the ruled as a mob of fickle and disorderly citizens whose rulers they obey only as they choose, and esteem only to the extent that they resemble themselves (562d). But in real-world democracies, Plato's Athens included, the citizen body includes the whole range of personalities and many working men called up in time of war fight no less well than full-time professionals. When finally, in book 9, it comes to tyranny, Plato assumes that a tyrant must have a personality which is the polar opposite of that of an aristocratic Philosopher-King, just as a tyrant's *polis* is the worst kind of society and a Philosopher-King's the best (576d). But Plato must have been well aware that real-life tyrants, some of whom he personally knew, are not all depraved criminals motivated by unbridled lusts. Quite the contrary: in the real world, a tyrant may well fit Thrasymachus's description of the unjust man who successfully plays to win precisely because his reason controls his passions and appetites to whatever extent is necessary if he is so to play his hand as to retain and augment his power.

Plato's typology of constitutions is, accordingly, impossible to take seriously if construed as what it purports to be. A possible rejoinder is that it shouldn't be so construed because it is no more than a diatribe about the abuse of power and the harm that it does both to rulers and to ruled. There was no lack of examples in Plato's world—to say nothing of human history between then and now—from which to point the moral that power corrupts. Moreover, the form which corruption takes is often related to the nature of the society's institutions and the norms and values associated with them: a timocratic society encourages *pleonexia* among brutal, ruthless, over-ambitious war leaders; an oligarchic society encourages *pleonexia* among an exclusive, venal, grasping elite; a democratic society encourages *pleonexia* among unprincipled, self-promoting, irresponsible demagogues; and in a society where a single person holds absolute power over the ruled, the tyrant cannot but be tempted to exercise that power for his own gratification without regard to the needs or wishes of the ruled. But what follows? The reader may share all of Plato's dislikes and fears. But they do nothing to enhance the persuasiveness of his advocacy of his just society in which the reader is asked to believe that internal conflict (*stasis*) will be eliminated, moderation (*sōphrosynē*) will prevail, rulers and ruled will share a common understanding of the behaviour appropriate to each, every citizen will refrain from *polypragmosynē*, and the educational system will ensure that no potentially subversive cultural innovation is ever admitted at all. The just society now looks less convincing than ever, for two reasons. First, Plato's dismissal of mixed constitutions prevents him from even considering the possibility that harmony and order, to the extent that they can be achieved, may depend on institutional arrangements which make deliberate provision against the risk that holders of power will abuse it. Second, he is further prevented from acknowledging this by his conviction that institutional change comes about through a change in the character of the individuals who occupy and perform their institutional roles rather than mutations in the practices which define those roles independently of who occupies them.

If, as many of the commentators believe, Plato shared what he says is the widespread admiration of the Spartan constitution, he presumably admired it for its success in curbing nonconformity, in fostering the soldierly virtues, in training the young to subordinate their personal interests to the interests of the state, and in freeing its warrior elite from any involvement in agricultural or artisan labour. He might even, given his willingness to allow selected women to be educated as Guardians, have approved of the greater freedom, including free-dom to own property, permitted to Spartan women as compared with Athenian women. But Sparta's relative freedom from *stasis*, by comparison with Athens and elsewhere, was in no way attributable to harmony be-tween its constituent parts. On the contrary: the sub-ordination of the Helots rested on what was officially represented as a state of war which legitimated their be-ing kept in their place by direct and uninhibited physi-cal coercion; and the harmony, such as it was, within the systact of Spartiate "equals" (*homoioi*) rested on a separation of powers and an inbuilt system of checks devised in explicit recognition of the need to restrain the pleonectic desire for riches, prestige, and political dominance which Sparta's distinctive educational sys-tem (the *agōgē*) was not able entirely to suppress. Plato will have known better than we do about the two he-reditary kings, the five elected ephors with their exten-sive judicial and executive powers, the common messes (*syssitia*) to which all Spartiates were required to con-tribute on pain of loss of civic rights, the free but in-ferior "dwellers-round-about" (*perioikoi*), and the secret police (*krypteia*) empowered to murder at will Helots thought to pose a danger to the state. He will also have known not only about the hubris and nemesis of Pausa-nias, the victor of Plataea, but about the conspiracy of an otherwise unknown Kinadon, narrated by Xenophon and referred to in passing by Aristotle, who was caught and punished by the ephors in about the year that Plato was thirty. He will also have known as well as we do that magistrates (*kosmoi*) in the Cretan *polis* of Dreros, for example, were expressly forbidden to hold annual office for ten years after their first year of tenure. There may be no point in reproaching him for not conducting an exercise in comparative political sociology of the kind that Aristotle was to do. But his deliberate refusal to extend his taxonomy of constitutions to cover kinds of whose existence he was fully aware, together with his failure to apply it to other than purely notional examples, means that it is of no help whatever to him in reinforcing his claims on behalf of the institutional design which, he claims, would guarantee harmony and order.

Successive commentators have been particularly baffled by what Plato has to say in *Republic* about democracy. It is widely supposed that he is venting his dislike of its workings as he experienced them in his own society during his own lifetime. Socrates' exchange with Glaucon at 562c–563e certainly reads as if they have in mind the here and now. Plato might, accordingly, have been expected to justify his dislike by showing that the vesting of judicial and executive power in the Athenian assembly (*ekklēsia*) has given rise to the inconsistencies in policy making, the compulsive litigiousness, the excessive licence in manners and mores, the popular envy of riches, the contempt for learning, and the mutual sycophancy of demagogues and populace which make

harmony and order unattainable. But he does not do
this. Instead, he presents the democratic *polis* as one in
which (he says) there is freedom for the individual citizen to rule or be ruled, to keep the peace or break it,
and to flout the rules (if there are any) about eligibility
for political or judicial office (557e–558a). This is so far
at variance with the actual state of affairs in any democratic *polis* as to make the reader wonder what Plato can
be getting at. But it looks as if the trouble is once again
that he wants to be able to say that the disharmony in
the *polis* is mirrored in the disharmony in the minds of
its typical citizens: the democratic man is all over the
place in his passing whims and self-indulgent fancies,
and the democratic society is all over the place in its
impermanent and short-sighted institutional arrangements. Sociologically speaking, it is not impossible that
undisciplined and irresponsible voters elect from among
themselves undisciplined and irresponsible rulers who
pursue undisciplined and irresponsible policies to the
detriment of the society as a whole. But the battle between the appetitive and the rational parts of the elec-
tors' minds (which, in a democratic society, Plato assumes
the appetitive part will always win) is not paralleled by
a battle between an appetitive and a rational part of the
polis. A democratic society like Athens (women and
slaves, as always, excluded) includes not only courageous
warriors dominated by passion but high-minded philosophers dominated by reason, of whom some may well,

politically speaking, be on the same democratic side. At the same time, its constitution provides for some strict and binding constraints on how philosophers, warriors, and producers are all to behave. Conformity is imposed by the *dēmos* in the modes of production, persuasion, and coercion alike. Litigious though the Athenians demonstrably were, the citizen-jurymen (*andres dikastoi*) to whom the orators addressed their pleas were there to enforce laws which the Assembly had passed. Plato may have disliked the laws and deplored the decisions that resulted from them. But the argument of book 8 of *Republic* does nothing to help persuade his readers to share his view of a hopelessly disparate and dissolute society of "drones" (564b) lurching into tyranny.

Greece and the territories adjoining it offered, in Plato's time, an abundance of evidence on which to base comparisons both about the rise and fall of constitutions of different kinds and about their relative capacity to maintain harmony and order. But if there is one conclusion which informed contemporary observers could not possibly have drawn from the world around them, it is that change from one constitution to another comes about in the way that Plato describes. The history of Athens, as Plato very well knew, was anything but a unilinear progression from timarchy to oligarchy to democracy to tyranny, just as the history of Sparta was anything but a decline into timocracy from an earlier aristocratic constitution supposedly approaching, even if not fully exemplifying, the Platonic ideal. Plato then makes matters worse by suggesting that timocracy arises out of aristocracy (545c) because the leaders (*hēgemones*), wise (*sophoi*) though they are (546a–b), are bound to make mistakes in the complex mathematical calculations necessary for the correct operation of the weird system of eugenics in which he appears seriously to believe. It is true that in the histories of the many different Greek *poleis* (and also tribal *ethnē*) of which he may be presumed to have had knowledge, there are examples of rulers or would-be rulers who approximate to his suggested kinds: there are timocratic generals, chrematistic oligarchs, crowd-pleasing demagogues, and murderous tyrants, as well as high-born members of close-knit governing clans, shrewd quasi-professional politicians, hereditary monarchs of more and less ability, and the occasional Solonic reformer whose proposals are put in place for the prospective benefit of both rulers and ruled. But Plato seems never to have realized that, important as the characters and abilities of individuals are to the singular, path-dependent histories of their own (and sometimes other) societies, lasting social change comes about through the competitive selection of alternative economic, ideological, and political practices which define the roles of which successive individuals are the incumbents. Nor does he seem ever to have realized that a mixture of practices can function to moderate rather than exacerbate internal dissension: a stable mode of production can be stable because it combines market with nonmarket practices, a stable mode of persuasion can be stable because it combines the practices of a hegemonic priesthood with those of licensed nonconformist sects, and a stable mode of coercion can be stable because it combines the practices of democratic election with those of oligarchic selection of officeholders by appointment rather than by vote or lot. Nor does he ever seem to have realized that social mobility can function to release the tensions which might otherwise lead to the formation of movements of dissent or rebellion led by aspirants to positions of power from which they feel themselves to be unfairly barred. Nor, finally, does he ever seem to have realized that what he would consider to be good, or at least stable, societies can be ruled by rulers whom he would consider bad, and vice versa.

Plato was not alone, then or since, in his distaste for what he saw as the irresponsibility of the Athenian *dēmos* (who had, after all, passed a death sentence on Socrates). Nor did he lack ample evidence for the seeming inability of the Greek *poleis* to avoid *stasis*, whether in the form of usurpations by, and depositions of, tyrants or of periodic outbreaks of violence between rich and poor. But when viewed from a more dispassionate and less moralistic perspective, the practices which defined the roles constitutive of Athenian democracy were remarkably resilient. Its short-lived overthrow in two violent coups at the close of the long war with Sparta would never have occurred if the war had by then been won, and on both occasions the restoration of democracy was accompanied by an amnesty. Historians of Greece have long been divided about the extent to which Athens's relative freedom from *stasis* following the establishment of democracy was due to its acquisition of an overseas empire and the diffusion of the rewards accruing from it among the *dēmos*. But when re-established after the overthrow of the "Thirty Tyrants," democracy remained unchallenged until the defeat of the Athenians by the Macedonians at the Battle of Chaeronea. Plato's prejudices made it impossible for him to draw from Athenian democracy, whatever its defects, the inference that if it were to be replaced by an unchallengeable oligarchy supported by an auxiliary police force from which the subordinated artisans, farmers, and businessmen were excluded, the ruled might resent the rulers more than ever.

By the end of book 10, which one far from wholly unsympathetic commentator calls "gratuitous," "clumsy," and "full of oddities," as well as including, in the purported proof of the immortality of the *psychē*, "one of the few really embarrassingly bad arguments in Plato,"[6] the reader is left with an institutional design which would require the Guardians, Auxiliaries, and Producers to have been indoctrinated in a way which his tripartite division of the human mind rules out. A possible

---

[6]Julia Annas, *An Introduction to Plato's Republic* (Oxford, 1987), pp. 335, 345.

rejoinder is to say that Plato was not, and knew very well that he was not, putting forward the kind of proposal that a real-life lawgiver (*nomothetēs*) might hope to see realized if the rulers of Athens (or anywhere else) were sufficiently attracted by his picture of an ideally harmonious and orderly society. Since he believes that a good society can only be good if its citizens are good, perhaps his aim was no more than to identify the virtues which they need to possess if social harmony and order are to be maintained. If only they were wise, courageous, temperate, and just, harmony and order would surely prevail. But why should they want to be just? Why should they not, as Thrasymachus expects them to do, apply such wisdom, courage, and temperance as they have to the pursuit of their selfish interests? Socrates continues to insist that the behaviour of a just person who is firmly and consistently disposed to be just is both good in itself and beneficial to the person so disposed. But he has not succeeded in demonstrating either. If Thrasymachus overstates his case, so equally does he. In the real world, egoistic and altruistic strategies are in constant competition, and neither drives the other to extinction. Some constitutional arrangements may provide a more favourable environment for the reproduction and diffusion of altruistic strategies than others do, and that may be one reason why some societies are freer from *stasis* for longer periods than others are. But even readers who are not as appalled as Popper was by the methods which Plato recommends have nowhere, in *Republic*, been given reason to believe that rulers of the kind that he would like to instal would have the smallest chance of success even if they did not, as Plato himself anticipates, start a succession of destructive quarrels among themselves.

Chapter Three

LEVIATHAN

1

No less than Plato, Hobbes sees the right education of the ruled by their rulers as critical to the maintenance of harmony and order. The people who are to do it are the "Publique Ministers" who have from the Sovereign "authority to teach, or to enable others to teach the people their duty to the Soveraign Power, and instruct them in the knowledge of what is just and unjust, thereby to render them more apt to live in godlinesse, and in peace amongst themselves" (p. 167). Unlike Plato, however, Hobbes believes that all of the Sovereign's subjects have the capacity to understand why it is that they should obey their Sovereign's commands for as long as the Sovereign is able to protect their lives and persons. He agrees with Plato that very few have "that skill of proceeding upon generall, and infallible rules, called Science" (p. 87), whose "theorems" have, for him, a function not unlike the function that the Form of the Good has for Plato. But as long as the Sovereign "has his Power entire," Hobbes thinks that there is no difficulty in instructing the people "in the Essential Rights (which are the Naturall and Fundamental Lawes) of Soveraignty." Failure can only be through the Sovereign's own fault or the fault of "those whom he trusteth in the administration of the Common-wealth" (p. 233). Like Plato, Hobbes sees passion and reason at odds with each other in the individual mind—without, in his case, being burdened by a forced analogy with conflict between different parts of the Commonwealth. But "justice," for Hobbes, is not about carrying out your duties in the station in life to which you have been assigned so much as about keeping your implied promise to obey your Sovereign. Like Plato, he is explicitly aware of going beyond the "ordinary definition" of justice as "*the constant Will of giving to every man his own*" (p. 101). But his definition of injustice is "no other than *the not Performance of covenant*" (p. 100).

As much, therefore, depends on getting the curriculum right for Hobbes as it does for Plato. The "Publique Ministers" need to do more than simply point out to their audiences that it is not sensible to disobey a Sovereign who holds a monopoly of the means of coercion. They must persuade them that they have an obligation to obey the commands of the Sovereign, whoever he, or she, or they may be; and from this it follows that Hobbes is bound to consider the kind and content of the religious instruction which the Sovereign is to permit or require. From the moment of its publication until the present day, the chapters on religion in *Leviathan* have provoked among the commentators reactions extending all the way from embarrassed evasion to indignant rebuttal. But there can be no doubt of their centrality to Hobbes's purpose, as he himself makes clear in the dedicatory epistle, where he says that although he is aware of the offence which his use of "certain texts of Holy Scripture" may cause, he has done it "with due submission, and also (in order to my Subject) necessarily; for they are the Outworks of the Enemy, from whence they impugne the Civill Power" (p. 3). There must be many readers of *Leviathan* who have found Hobbes's elaborate citations and exegeses of selected passages of both the Old and New Testaments as disconcerting as many readers of *Republic* have found Plato's eugenics. Understandable as they may be in the context of what he saw as the need to take issue with the pernicious theological doctrines and spurious claims to temporal power of both Catholics on one side and Protestants on the other, a seemingly obsessional preoccupation with recasting the Christian conceptions of the Garden of Eden, Moses and the Prophets, the teachings of Jesus, and (most eccentrically of all) the afterlife can only detract from the persuasiveness of what he has to say about power, freedom, sovereignty, and political obligation. But what Hobbes saw around him was not

only the threat which is always and everywhere posed to
the stability of a society by the three "principall causes
of quarrel" which are in the "nature of man": "Competition, Diffidence and Glory" (p. 88)—or, as we might
put it, greed, fear, and pride. He also saw around him
how social stability can be undermined not merely by
unscrupulous pursuit of material gain, political power,
and public prestige but by doctrines "repugnant to Civil
Society" (p. 223), of which some of the most dangerous
are precisely those which appeal to what purport to be
either the truths of established religion or direct revela-
tions from God. Superstition can do as much damage to
a Commonwealth as selfishness can.

That proposition is another of those to which, like
Plato's insistence that power should be in the hands of
those best qualified to exercise it, no reader is likely to
take immediate objection as it stands. But how is superstition to be banished from the minds of the Sovereign's
Subjects? What is to replace it? And how can it be prevented from reemerging in some new and equally insid-
ious form? To the question whether Hobbes's proposals
for the instruction of the ruled have any realistic prospect of achieving their objective, the answer must be
no. They are almost as unconvincing as Plato's. Hobbes
does not share Plato's futile hope of stopping cultural
evolution dead in its tracks. By comparison with Plato,
he is almost a pluralist. Although "we are to remember,
that the Right of Judging what Doctrines are fit for

Peace, and to be taught to the Subjects, is in all Com-
mon-wealths inseparably annexed (as hath already been
proved cha.18.) to the Soveraign Power Civill" (p. 372),
he is ready to allow for some innocuous differences of
opinion among Christians. But he has no good argument to show either why the "Publique Ministers" can
be assumed to be successful in inculcating lessons that
the Sovereign wishes them to teach or why the Subjects
should not continue to be receptive to other ones.

In chapter 30, Hobbes identifies the Universities as
the "Means and Conduits" by which the people are to
be instructed in justice and injustice, and at the very
end of *Leviathan* he says that he thinks that his Dis-
course "may be profitably printed, and more profitably
taught in the Universities, in case they also think so, to
whom the judgment of the same belongeth," by which
means "the most men, knowing their Duties, will be the
less subject to serve the Ambition of a few discontented
persons, in their purposes against the State" (p. 491).
But he is at the same time all too aware not only that
"the Passions of men, are more commonly potent than
their Reason" (p. 131) but that the Universities were the
places at which were educated the preachers, lawyers,
and others who maintained doctrines subversive of the
power of the King even though "Doctrine repugnant to
Peace, can no more be True, than Peace and Concord
can be against the Law of Nature" (p. 125). Once, therefore, "SCIENCE, that is, Knowledge of Consequences,

which is called also PHILOSOPHY" (p. 61) is being properly taught, everything will be all right. But will it? Philosophers, however superior their intellectual capacities
to those of the people at large, are equally prone to be
motivated by their passions rather than their reason, and
universities, whatever syllabus their governing authori-
ties prescribe, will always offer opportunities for discussion, debate, and criticism of received wisdom. Hobbes
is vehemently opposed to the exercise of "private judgements" which lead subjects to challenge what they have
been taught by reference to their individual consciences.
But he is being as naive as Plato if he believes that it
could be prevented if their instruction was in the hands
of right-thinking philosophers or jurists who would
convince their pupils that the arguments of *Leviathan*
are as well founded as mathematical proofs.

Equally damaging is Hobbes's failure to consider the
potential for dissent which is inherent in the structure
of any society where the unequal distribution of power
creates a perceived identity of interest among groups or
categories of subjects collectively denied what they regard as their legitimate share of their society's resources.
He thinks that "They whom necessity, or covetousnesse
keepeth attent on their trades, and labour" are thereby
"diverted from the deep meditation, which the learning
of truth, not onely in the matter of Natural Justice, but
also of all other Sciences necessarily requireth" (pp. 236-
237). There is a whiff of Plato here in the implication

that the artisans, farmers, and businessmen are not, after
all, as educable as their social superiors. But however
untutored they may be in Science, some of them are
well capable of articulating reasoned objections to the
disabilities to which they are subjected. Hobbes never
refers, as Clarendon does in arguing against him,[1] to Wat
Tyler and the Peasants' Revolt. But the indication in
chapter 22 is that he would be likely to assign any combination of employees joined together for the purpose
of extracting higher wages from their employers to the
category of "Private Bodies, Regular, but Unlawfull"
such as "Corporations of Beggars, Theeves, and Gipsies"
who "unite themselves into one person Representative
. . . the better to order their trade of begging and stealing"
(p. 163). Whether or not he would regard trade unions as
on a par with beggars and thieves, he seems seriously to
suppose that any "person Representative" who is arguing a case for better treatment on behalf of oppressed
and exploited labourers will be persuaded that they
are not even authorized to suggest the possibility that
they are being unjustly treated because, by the authority they have bestowed on their Sovereign, they have
forfeited the right to speak ill of him. Hobbes knows
perfectly well that under any form of government there
will be some subjects who will believe themselves to be

---

[1] In *A Brief View of the Dangerous and Pernicious Errors to Church and State in Mr. Hobbes's Book Entitled Leviathan*, quoted in S. A. Lloyd, *Ideals as Interests in Hobbes's* Leviathan: *The Power of Mind over Matter* (Cambridge, 1992), p. 377.

"oppressed by the Governours" (p. 130). But the answer he gives to anyone who complains that "the Condition of Subjects is very miserable" is that "the estate of Man can never be without some incommodity or other," that such incommodity is "scarce sensible" by comparison with the horrors of civil war, that "Soveraign Governours" derive no pleasure or profit from "the dammage, or weakening of their Subjects" on whom their own "strength and glory' depends, and that it is the subjects" own "restiveness" which makes it necessary for their Governours "to draw from them what they can in time of Peace, that they may have means on any emergent occasion, or sudden need, to resist, or take advantage of their Enemies" (pp. 128-129).

The trouble with this as an argument by which to pacify Wat Tyler or anyone else representing the oppressed is, as one commentator after another has pointed out, that the currently oppressed will at once, and incontrovertibly, reply that they have never in fact covenanted with their Sovereign to obey him in return for protection against a reversion to the war of all against all. It is true that the mythical State of Nature has generated much subtle and illuminating discussion about the form of agreement into which rational persons would enter in a primordial pre-political world. But Hobbes's theory that the members of subsequent generations not party to the initial agreement have tacitly consented to obey the Sovereign under whom they find themselves is plausibly dismissed by one commentator as not merely a failure but a "dismal" one.[2] Hobbes could fairly claim that it is a matter of sociological fact that most people, most of the time, conform to the practices which define the roles by which their society's economic, ideological, and political institutions are constituted, and that they believe, or at least appear to believe, that the day-to-day workings of those institutions make it worth their while to do so. But he wants to convince those who feel oppressed by their rulers that if they are not willing to accept any and all of the "incommodities" short of violation of the Laws of Nature which their rulers impose on them, they will plunge their whole society into a world in which every man behaves like a Thrasymachean egoist and every mutual understanding on which once stable-seeming institutions rested will be dissolved. This is simply not true, and the oppressed know very well that it isn't. Under some sociological conditions, perhaps, an initially isolated act of insubordination in the mode of coercion can prompt a nationwide mutiny, or an initial breach of contract in the mode of production set off an accelerating spiral of reciprocal defection, or a single heretical manifesto in the mode of persuasion incite wholesale apostasy. But under any form of government, it is a commonplace occurrence for challenges

[2] Gregory S. Kavka, *Hobbesian Moral and Political Theory* (Princeton, 1986), p. 398.

to be mounted by some group or category of the ruled against their rulers, and whether the rulers accede to their demands or refuse them, the society's institutions continue to function much as before. Hobbes may not think that the doctrine of obedience to the Sovereign which he would like the Sovereign's Publique Ministers to teach is a Platonic lie, but it might as well be; and those Ministers have no more chance of instilling it, whether directly or through the university-educated clerics, lawyers, and gentry, into the heads of the population at large than Plato's Guardians would have of instilling into the heads of the Auxiliaries and Producers his fantastic "Phoenician" story about putting gold into those born capable of ruling, silver into their auxiliaries, and a mixture of iron and copper into the rest.

2

Hobbes does not, in any case, suppose for a moment that the Sovereign's control of the means of persuasion, however skilfully deployed, will remove the need to retain a monopoly of the means of coercion and be ready to use force as and when intra-societal disorder or the inter-societal State of Nature may require. Whatever his hopes for what the right education of the populace might achieve in reconciling them to their rulers, he does not believe that harmony and order can be achieved and sustained without the Fear which, except in the case of "some generous natures," is "the onely thing, (when there is appearance of profit, or pleasure by breaking the Lawes,)" that makes men keep their promises (p. 206). It will always be the case that "every man by nature seeketh his own benefit, and promotion" (p. 133), that "the proper object of every mans Will, is some Good to himselfe" (p. 176), and that "the naturall Passions of men, when there is no visible Power to keep them in awe, and tye them to the performance of their Covenants, and observation of those Lawes of Nature set down in the fourteenth and fifteenth Chapters" would without that make impossible their escape from the "miserable condition of Warre" (p. 117). Under any form of government, therefore, the Sovereign will have work to do. Whether the Commonwealth is a monarchy, an aristocracy, or a democracy, "either One, or More, or All, must have the Soveraign Power (which I have shewn to be indivisible) entire" (p. 129). But must it?

No commentator, so far as I can discover, has answered that question with an unqualified yes. Hobbes's absolutism (if that is the right word for it) is more sympathetically discussed by some than by others, often depending on whether they think it unworkable on the one hand or unnecessary on the other. But Hobbes does not help himself by the way in which he justifies ostensibly empirical sociological generalizations by recourse to pre-emptive definitions. Part 1 of *Leviathan* ("Of Man") is full of definitions, and Hobbes himself is constantly remarking how the different names used for the same things by different people are reflections of their different opinions and tastes—a "tyranny" is simply a monarchy which the speaker dislikes, and so on. But what follows? It is one thing to say that a ruler with less than a total monopoly of power is not properly speaking a "Sovereign": thus, Hobbes says that "if the King bear the person of the People, and the generall Assembly bear also the person of the People, and another Assembly bear the person of a Part of the People, they are not one Person, nor one Soveraign, but three Persons, and three Soveraigns" (p. 228). But it is another thing to predict that no such ruler will remain a ruler for long. Hobbes claims in the concluding paragraph of chapter 21 that "In those Nations, whose Commonwealths have been long-lived, and not been destroyed, but by forraign warre, the Subjects never did dispute of the Soveraign Power" (p. 145). This, however, invites the immediate response that the historical record is full of counter-examples.[3] Is Hobbes saying that the rulers of long-lived Commonwealths who were not absolute Sovereigns in his sense have never had to put down a rebellion and done so with success, which is demonstrably

[3] As one generally sympathetic commentator puts it, "Given that, prior to Hobbes's day, governments that certainly looked like aristocracies and democracies had existed and survived as well as any absolute monarchy, the arguments we have reconstructed on Hobbes's behalf that they are 'impossible' looks a bit foolish, to say the least." Jean Hampton, *Hobbes and the Social Contract Tradition* (Cambridge, 1986), p. 106.

false? Or is he saying only that in no long-lived Commonwealth have rebellious subjects ever successfully overthrown their ruling Sovereign, which is true but trivial?

Hobbes's claim to have shown that sovereignty is indivisible is best construed as a summary statement of his belief that rulers who are so imprudent as to share control of the means of coercion with another institutional agency will sooner or later find the power they have handed over turned against them: hence his quotation of the saying "*a Kingdome divided in it selfe cannot stand*" (p. 127; cf. p. 227), his insistence that "Powers divided mutually destroy each other" (p. 225), and his warning of how serious an error it is for a man seeking "*to obtain a Kingdome*" to be "*content with lesse Power, than to the Peace, and defence of the Common-wealth is necessarily required*" (p. 222). A wise ruler will sometimes delegate power but never share it, and although willing to listen to advice, will never allow the adviser the power of decision. To share power is to forfeit it, and once forfeited it will not be regained. If there is not a single final adjudicator of disputes and enforcer of the sanctions by which the adjudication is underwritten, the "Civill Lawes" will lose their hold over the ruled. But these are no more than prudential maxims, or warnings to rulers of what may befall them if they fail to follow Hobbes's advice. They are not empirical generalizations—or if they are, they are very obviously invalid ones.

Leviathan never examines the possibility that a separation of powers, far from increasing the risk of internal disorder, might under some conditions diminish it. The idea of a loyal opposition—that is, an alternative government-in-waiting which could replace the existing rulers within an unchanged set of economic, ideological, and political institutions—is never mentioned. Not only is an opposition, for Hobbes, disloyal by definition, but a faction or party licensed by an existing government to bid to replace it must, by its very existence, compromise the willingness of the ruled to obey the present one. Hobbes does have a valid point to make when he addresses the thorny question of succession: as the previous history of England had shown many times over, it is when the succession to the monarchy is disputed that the Commonwealth is most in danger of civil war, and if the "Multitude" is left "without any Soveraign at all," every man will "submit himselfe to such as he thinks best able to protect him; or if he can, protect himselfe by his owne sword" (p. 136). But Hobbes does not properly consider whether the risk of descent into civil war might be less under a constitution which affords at least some of the "multitude" the opportunity to choose between rival contenders for the topmost political role or roles without recourse to arms. Nor does he assess the potential for greater stability under a constitution which separates the mode of persuasion from the mode of coercion, so that an English King

(or Queen) and Archbishop, or a Japanese Tennō and
Shōgun, or an Indian Brahman and Kshatriya, can control separate areas of social space and collaborate across
the institutional frontier between them. They must, of
course, be willing to collaborate: for as long as the Pope
tries to dominate the Emperor, or the Emperor the Pope,
a Hobbesian state of war will persist between them. But
a separation of powers will not inevitably provoke or
escalate internal disorder in circumstances where a Sovereign meeting Hobbes's requirement of indivisibility
would moderate or suppress it.

There is, moreover, the other meaning of the word
"representation"—the representation of the interests
of one or more groups or categories of subjects not
merely through the "Counsell" given on their behalf to
the Sovereign as the "Representative person of a Common-wealth" (p. 179) but through their participation as
of constitutional right in decisions of national policy.
Here is Macaulay speaking in the House of Commons
in a debate on parliamentary reform: "In all ages a chief
cause of the intestine disorder of states has been that the
natural distribution of power and the legal distribution
of power have not corresponded with one another."
The extension of the franchise to give a voice to under-
represented interests is not, of course, a proposal with
topical relevance to the condition of England when
Hobbes was composing *Leviathan*. But I have quoted
Macaulay's speech because in it he goes on to say, "This

is no newly discovered truth. It was known to Aristotle more than two thousand years ago." No reader of *Leviathan* can have failed to notice Hobbes's insistent hostility to Aristotle, who as well as being guilty in his *Metaphysics* of maintaining propositions than which "scarce anything can be more absurdly said in naturall Philosophy" (p. 461), "puts it down in his *Politiques*, (lib.6.cap.2) *In democracy*, Liberty *is to be supposed: for 'tis commonly held, that no man is* Free *in any other Government*" (p. 150). But leaving aside, for the moment, Hobbes's own pre-emptive definition of freedom, an assembly in which representatives of different interest groups can argue their case before it is put to the vote can leave the dissentients less disposed to make trouble if the decision goes against them than they would be if excluded from making representations to the sovereign person or body other than by indirect access through intermediaries not chosen by themselves. Hobbes recognizes that a Monarch can be seduced by the "evil Counsell" of a favourite or flatterer but thinks the danger greater in an Assembly where there are more people who "becoming one an others Flatterers, serve one anothers Covetousnesse and Ambition by turnes" (p. 132). But an Assembly whose members are there because they are mandated by their constituents might be more, not less, prone to seditious designs if they could not represent their constituents' interests in the body where the power of decision resides.

Still less does Hobbes consider seriously the possibility that Covenants without the Sword, which "are but Words, and of no strength to secure a man at all" (p. 117), might be made and kept independently of the coercive sanctions attaching to the roles of the Sovereign and his agents. He allows that it can sometimes be pride, rather than fear, which motivates someone who has made a covenant to hold to it—as he puts it, "a Glory, or Pride in appearing not to need to breake it" (p. 99). In this, he might be read as anticipating game-theoretic discussions of the handicap effect and the gain to players who are able to enhance their competitive position by showing their willingness to act to their seeming disadvantage. But he then goes on to say that such "Generosity" is "too rarely found to be presumed on." He does not appreciate the extent to which the desire for personal prestige, coupled with strong reciprocity, can make reputation as powerful an incentive to cooperation as fear of coercive sanctions. This to some extent reflects the relative lack of attention given in *Leviathan* to economic, as opposed to ideological and political, relations of power. Hobbes is well aware of Commonwealths that have "not onely maintained, but also encreased their Power, partly by the labour of trading from one place to another, and partly by selling the Manifactures, whereof the Materials were brought in from other place" (p. 171). But he does not allow for the extent to which markets can function in a harmonious and orderly manner through the sharing of information about who can be trusted and who can't. For Hobbes, "to assigne in what places, and for what commodities, the Subject shall traffique abroad, belongeth to the Soveraign," and the danger which concerns him is that if discretion is left to "private persons," some "would bee drawn for gaine, both to furnish the enemy with means to hurt the Common-wealth, and hurt it themselves, by importing such things, as pleasing mens appetites, be nevertheless noxious, or at least unprofitable to them" (p. 173). In this, he is right to the extent that no government can afford to allow markets to operate entirely beyond the reach of the law. But the law, with the Sovereign's control of the means of coercion behind it, is not the only sanction by which the pleonectic for gain can be restrained. "*Pecuniary Punishment*," as Hobbes calls it, by which the offender can be deprived by the Sovereign not only of "a Summe of Mony, but also of Lands, or any other goods which are usually bought and sold for mony" (p. 217), may on occasion be the most appropriate and effective method. But strong reciprocators who will ostracize not only the covenant breakers but those who refuse to do likewise can be equally effective in ensuring that buyers and sellers, borrowers and lenders, and projectors and investors all adhere sufficiently to the agreements into which they have entered for enforcement by the Sovereign not to be required.

Hobbes equally fails to consider the possibility of institutional mechanisms by which individuals using common-pool resources can come together to solve problems of collective action without needing to involve an agency of the Sovereign. He sees the "NUTRITION of a Common-wealth" as consisting in "the *Plenty*, and *Distribution* of *Materials* conducing to Life," which when "concocted" are conveyed "by convenient conduits, to the Publique use," and Plenty as depending "(next to Gods favour) meerly on the labour and industry of men" (p. 170). To the extent that this gives rise to rival claims of possession, they are for the Sovereign to resolve, since in the "Division of the Land" the Sovereign "assigneth to every man a portion, according as he, and not according as any Subject, or any number of them, shall judge agreeable to Equity, and the Common Good" (p. 171). Some latter-day economists and ecologists have agreed with Hobbes that "because of the tragedy of the commons, environmental problems cannot be solved through co-operation . . . and the rationale for government with major coercive powers is overwhelming," and that "even if we avoid the tragedy of the commons, it will only be by recourse to the tragic necessity of Leviathan."[4] But Elinor Ostrom shows, with the help of both game-theoretic models and empirical case studies, that contracting parties who have set themselves to obtain long-term collective benefits from

---

[4] W. Ophuls, *Ecology and the Politics of Scarcity* (San Francisco, 1977), pp. 228, 229, quoted in Elinor Ostrom, *Governing the Commons: The Evolution of Institutions for Collective Action* (Cambridge, 1990), pp. 8-9.

common-pool resources such as forests, meadows, or fisheries can make credible commitments without external coercion. Hobbes cannot accept that there are co-ordination problems which can be solved by agreements between self-interested parties who come together without prior commitment, because that would fatally weaken his argument that their only possible escape from a State of Nature is by authorisation of a Sovereign to whom they surrender their autonomy. Admittedly, not all institutions established by such agreements survive and prosper. Hobbes's "natural Passions of men" each seeking his own benefit are such that they will always be at risk from the intransigent dispositions and duplicitous designs of defectors, free-riders, and cheats. But many do. It is simply not true to say of two parties who have committed themselves to collaboration for a common purpose that there must always be "a common Power set over them both, with right and force sufficient to compel performance" (p. 96).

Hobbes's difficulty, as many commentators have observed, is that he wants to be sure that the Sovereign has the power to deter disaffected Subjects from rebellion but recognizes that Subjects will not be bound to unconditional obedience where the Sovereign fails to protect them as the "Law of Nature," which is "the Eternall Law of God" (p. 192), entitles them to demand. Although, therefore, the Sovereign can put his Subjects to death, he cannot require them to kill themselves or others (p. 151); and although "To resist the Sword of the Commonwealth, in defence of another man, guilty, or innocent, no man hath Liberty" (p. 152), if a man is interrogated by the Sovereign about a crime he has himself committed, "he is not bound (without assurance of Pardon) to confesse it" (p. 151). Hobbes sees that the preservation of harmony and order is more likely to be achieved in a society where the subjects have some protection against the possibility that the Sovereign will commit "Iniquity" as opposed to "Injustice, or Injury in the proper signification" (p. 124). But once there are some commands which, if the Sovereign issues them, they are not required to obey, the door has been opened to disaffected subjects who will argue that some of the Sovereign's actions are in breach of the Law of Nature. This might not matter if Hobbes could vindicate his claim to have provided "geometricall" proof of the conclusions which he draws from the premise of a hypothetical State of Nature and the Contract which any rational person would have signed up to. It would be enough for it to have been proved to the Subjects that their prudential self-interest lies in behaving as Hobbes wishes them to behave and refraining from arguing the terms of the Contract or seeking to replace their present Sovereign with another. When, however, he requires the Subjects to be taught "not to affect change of Government," it transpires that they are to be taught "that they *ought not* [my italics] to be in love with any forme of Government they see in their neighbour Nations, more than with their own, nor (whatsoever present prosperity they behold in Nations that are otherwise governed than they,) to desire change" (p. 233). It is true that this moral injunction is supplemented by a prudential warning that "they that go about by disobedience, to doe no more than reforme the Common-wealth, shall find they do thereby destroy it" (p. 234). But this warning is then supplemented in turn by a reminder that "This desire of change, is like the breach of the first of Gods Commandments: For there God sayes, *Non habebis Deos alienos*." Moreover, the subjects are to be taught that "not onely the unjust facts, but the designs and intentions to do them, (though by accident hindred,) are Injustice; which consisteth in the pravity of the will, as well as in the irregularity of the act" (p. 236). When, in the chapter on "the RIGHTS of Soveraignes by Institution," Hobbes says that "they that are subjects to a Monarch, cannot without his leave cast off Monarchy" (p. 122), he cannot mean that they cannot; what he means is that they ought not, because to do so is to break their Covenant, which "is injustice." Whatever force these arguments may have, it is not the force of mathematical or "geometrical" proof—so much so, indeed, that Hobbes might plausibly be accused in the terms in which he accuses others of "betraying their want of right Reason, by the claym they lay to it" (p. 33).

Sovereigns, however, have another means to hand if they wish to guard themselves against the risk of deposition at the hands of disaffected Subjects, and that is to behave in such a way as to remove the cause of the disaffection. They can, so to speak, bend over backwards to make sure that they conform to the proviso in the Contract that they are to respect the Laws of Nature. Hobbes appears to assume that that is what a prudent and sensible Sovereign will do. He will wish to be "reverenced and beloved of his People" (pp. 243–244); he will see to it that "Justice be equally administred to all degrees of People" (p. 237); he will provide for, and not leave to the "Charity of private persons," those who "by accident inevitable, become unable to maintain themselves by their labour" (p. 239); and he will see that "the end of punishing is not revenge, and discharge of choler; but correction, either of the offender, or of others by his example" (p. 240). Hobbes even goes so far as explicitly to deny that "A Law may be conceived to be Good, when it is for the benefit of the Soveraign; though it be not Necessary for the People" on the grounds that "the good of the Soveraign and People, cannot be separated" (p. 240). But at this point, Thrasymachus would not be able to restrain himself from breaking in with another of his saloon-bar tirades. Bullshit! We all know perfectly well how rulers actually behave. They treat their subjects well only where they see it as helping them to retain their power or, better still, to increase it. Indeed, Hobbes himself agrees with Thrasymachus that "Kings, whose power is greatest, turn their endeavours to the assuring of it at home by Lawes, or abroad by Wars: and when that is done, there succeedeth a new desire; in some, of Fame from new Conquest; in others of ease and sensuall pleasure; in others, of admiration, or being flattered for excellence in some art, or other ability of the mind" (p. 70). Kings, in other words, are motivated just as their potentially unruly subjects are by Competition, Diffidence, and Glory. Some fortunate people may live in a Commonwealth where the Sovereign has decided that his power can most effectively be retained and increased by improving the condition of the People. But just look at all the monarchs, dictators, tyrants, despots, and emperors who haven't!

Hobbes has no adequate answer to the Deioces Problem. According to Herodotus, Deioces became King of the Medes by establishing a reputation as an impartial and trustworthy mediator and then refusing to continue unless given a bodyguard and a palace, after which he behaved just as Thrasymachus would predict. To Hobbes, the Medes could have no reason to be disaffected provided that Deioces used the power entrusted to him and his soldiers to keep them in peace and safety. Hobbes's Sovereigns, like Plato's Guardians, must have their Auxiliaries if they are to maintain the control of the means of coercion which they need to ensure harmony and order. The Medes may dislike the ways in which they are treated by Deioces and his henchmen and resent the perquisites and privileges which they enjoy, but if they rebel they will merely provoke a war of all against all from which their only relief will be to agree to hand power to another Sovereign who, they hope, will behave better towards them than Deioces did. But the dilemma is of Hobbes's own making. It has nothing to do with whether or not the Medes have an obligation to obey Deioces or a right to resist his commands. It is simply not true that they had no choice but to concede him the monopoly of power that they did on the terms for which he asked. Nor is it true that the alternative was a war of all against all. The sociological—or if you prefer, palaeoanthropological—fact is that in a pre-political world, although the motives of Competition, Diffidence, and Glory are ever present, the pleonectic of gain are restrained by vigilant monitoring and compulsory sharing, the pleonectic of prestige by ridicule and ostracism, and the pleonectic of physical power by counter-dominant coalitions. Yes, there are bullies, braggarts, thieves, murderers, self-aggrandizers, free-riders, and cheats. But it is not Hobbes's mythical State of Nature any more than it is Rousseau's, and it did not require a Hobbesian Sovereign for there to be harmony and order sufficient to keep together the hunting and foraging bands from whose members we are all descended.

3

It is in chapter 21 of *Leviathan* on "the Liberty of Subjects" that Hobbes's recourse to pre-emptive definition most clearly exposes the weakness of his argument. He has no difficulty in repudiating his republican opponents' claim that under a monarchy, the Sovereign's Subjects are no more than slaves. In an oligarchy, where sovereignty is in a council of state, or a democracy, where it is in a popular assembly, the degree of liberty enjoyed by the Subjects is equally at the Sovereign's discretion. Just as a monarch can allow them "the Liberty to buy, and sell, and otherwise contract with one another; to chose their own aboad, their own diet, their own trade of life, and institute their children as they themselves think fit; & the like" (p. 148), so can a democratic assembly deprive them of whatever liberties they previously enjoyed and impose a tyranny as repressive as any single ruler could do. At the same time, subjects are as free under a monarchy as under a democracy to resist as strongly as they are physically able to do when their lives and persons are under threat. But Hobbes knows that he must say more than this if he is to controvert his opponents. In chapter 5 ("Of Reason, and Science") he says that it is as "Absurd" for a man to talk of being "*Free*" in terms other than "hindered by opposition" as to talk of "a *round Quadrangle*; or accidents of *Bread* in *Cheese*" (p. 34). But this is a giveaway. Someone who takes issue with the definition of freedom as the absence of physical constraint is not in the same position as someone who takes issue with a definition of circularity which rules out quadrangles. It is Hobbes, if anyone, who is being absurd.

If there is one passage in *Leviathan* which reveals more clearly than any other why Hobbes is driven to define liberty as he does, it is the sentence about the "Turrets of the city of *Luca*" on which is written "in great characters at this day, the word LIBERTAS; yet no man can thence inferre, that a particular man has more Libertie, or Immunitie from the service of the Commonwealth there, than in *Constantinople*" (p. 149). To many readers then and since, the suggestion that the citizens of Lucca are no freer than the subjects of a Turkish Sultan is, indeed, absurd. Harrington, in his *Oceana*, pointedly charged Hobbes with failing to distinguish liberty *by* the Laws from liberty *from* the Laws: neither the Lucchese nor the Turk has the second, but the Lucchese has much more than the Turk does of the first.[5] Hobbes, however, knows perfectly well that a Lucchese is better able to lead his life as he pleases than a Turk. In his terms, the difference is not one of freedom but of power. As he goes on himself to say, the "Libertie to do, or forebeare, according to his own [the Subject's] discretion," is "in some places more, and in some lesse" (p. 152). But he cannot be construed as voicing no more than a terminological preference. His opponents are subjects who will justify the taking up of arms against their established Sovereign in the name of liberty, and Hobbes is

---

[5] James Harrington, "*The Commonwealth of Oceana*" and "*A System of Politics*," ed. J.G.A. Pocock (Cambridge, 1992), p. 20.

concerned above all to prevent them from doing so. Once they have successfully rebelled, and the power of life and death has thereby passed from one Sovereign to another, the Subjects are in the same relation to the new one as to the old (as Hobbes himself was when he submitted himself to a new one by returning to England in the year after *Leviathan* was published). But behind all the quibbling (as Thrasymachus would call it) over the definition of Liberty is Hobbes's constant fear that if he fails to win the argument, there will be mounting danger that unruly subjects incited by imagined griev- ances and irrational superstitions will provoke internal disorder leading to civil war.

The reason for which he has to hold fast to his pre- emptive definition of Liberty is that he cannot afford to acknowledge that to concede the demand that rulers should be answerable to the ruled for how they rule them might actually improve the chances of harmony and order. Aristotle, as it happens, set it out clearly in his discussion of tyranny when he said of his third type of tyrant, who rules over men as good or better than he to his own advantage and against their will, that he is "unaccountable" (*anypeuthunos*) and that that is why no free man will willingly put up with it (*Politics* 1295a). Aristotle makes the point in moralistic as well as so- ciological terms. But the sociological point is that men who think of themselves as the equals of their rulers will need not only to approve of whatever methods of

appointment and succession place the rulers in their
roles but also to be satisfied that there is some inde-
pendent institutional mechanism whereby their performance in their roles can be assessed. As Aristotle well
knew, the holders of public office in Athens were subject to audit (*euthynai*) at the expiry of their term as well
as scrutiny of their credentials (*dokimasia*) beforehand.
Hobbes can repeat as often and as forcibly as he pleases
that the Athenians are mistaken in their idea of what it
means to be free and that such licence as is permitted to
them by Athenian law could be revoked by decision of
their assembly as readily as by a tyrant. They do not need
to be reminded where it is that sovereignty lies under
their constitution. It is because their constitution gives
them as individual citizens such powers of appointment
and assessment as it does that they are more willing to
obey the laws which their assembly has passed than they
are willing, except under compulsion, to obey a tyrant's
decrees. Hobbes may then tell them that a tyrant is not
restricting their freedom to disobey for as long as he
does not put them literally in chains. But that will not
reconcile them to his rule. They want a power to restrain him, should they wish to, such as they have over
the holders of public office in Athens.

There is considerable debate among the commentators about Hobbes's attitude to democracy, just as there
is about Plato's. Since the State of Nature is one where
every individual confronts every other in a relationship

of primordial equality, and the Covenant which generates a Commonwealth is "of every man with every man" (p. 120), Hobbes's Sovereign could be said to owe his legitimacy to a process of democratic decision making. But this hardly makes Hobbes a democrat. The "Soveraign Power" carried by the "*One Person, of whose Acts a great Multitude, by mutuall Covenants one with another, have made themselves every one the Author*" (p. 121) is brought into being in order to prevent a regression to the war of all against all, which the Covenant brings to an end. It is true that Hobbes never denies that a democratic assembly, like an oligarchic council of state, can be the "One Person" whose power protects the lives and persons of those subject to it, and that his dislike is principally of demagogues and their "motly orations" (p. 181). But the reader of *Leviathan* is left in no doubt that he thinks monarchy the preferable form of government. Dissenting opinions voiced by rival demagogues may not always be seditious or treasonable. But whereas a Monarch "cannot disagree with himselfe, out of envy, or interest," an Assembly "may; and that to such a height, as may produce a Civill Warre," (p. 132).

The trouble now is that Hobbes's arguments in favour of monarchy are no stronger than Plato's in favour of an oligarchy of Guardians. The proposition that a single ruler cannot disagree with himself is another of those that is true only by pre-emptive definition. Hobbes acknowledges, as I have already remarked, no less readily than Plato that passion and reason can be at war with each other within the same person's mind, and if that person is a ruler, the outcome in government policy may bear directly on the well-being of the ruled. A monarch can be no less hesitant, indecisive, and easily swayed by conflicting advice than a council of state or an assembly. Hobbes assumes that a monarch can, but an assembly cannot, receive "counsell . . . with as much secrecy as he will" (p. 131). But that is not so. An assembly can meet in closed session to hear a confidential report, and although a monarch can, if he so chooses, be the sole recipient of one, there will always be the risk that as others become, as they will have to, privy to its contents, confidentiality may be breached in no different a way than if it is breached by a member of an assembly. Hobbes evidently believes that a decision taken by a single person is likely to be wiser than one taken by a "multitude."[6] But he makes no attempt to offer evidence for his belief.

Weakest of all Hobbes's arguments in favour of monarchy is that "in Monarchy, the private interest is the same with the publique" (p. 131). This is as obviously untrue as his more general claim that the good of

[6] Keith Hoekstra, "A Lion in the House: Hobbes and Democracy" in Annabel Brett and James Tully, eds., *Rethinking the Foundations of Modern Political Thought* (Cambridge, 2006), p. 199 n. 43, cites Hobbes's own autobiographical remark that he learned from Thucydides how much one man's wisdom exceeds that of a crowd (*"quantum coetu sapit unus homo"*).

the Sovereign and of the People cannot be separated. Hobbes gives as his reason that "The riches, power, and honour of a Monarch arise onely from the riches, strength, and reputation of his Subjects," whereas "in a Democracy, or Aristocracy, the publique prosperity conferres not so much to the private fortune of one that is corrupt, or ambitious, as doth many times a perfidious advice, a treacherous action, or a Civill warre." But again, he offers no evidence in support of this generalization, and it would be easy to draw from the historical record counter-examples which tell against it. In any case, even if Hobbes could show that the corrupt or ambitious are more likely to pursue their quest for power by illegitimate self-enrichment under a monarchy, but by illegitimate political intrigue under a democracy or an aristocracy, that would not make any more plausible the claim that in a monarchy the private and the public interest are everywhere and always more closely allied.

Readers of *Leviathan* who want as much as Hobbes does to live in a harmonious and orderly society, and fear as much as he does the prospect that disaffection, if unchecked, will bring about a regression to anarchy, will no doubt agree with him that the price to be paid is submission to a ruler whose laws are underwritten by coercive sanctions. But they are not thereby committed to agreeing with him either that power needs to be concentrated to the degree for which he argues in a single Sovereign or that the Sovereign needs to be immunized to the degree for which he argues from criticism or protest. No amount of special pleading by the commentators can rescue Hobbes from having failed twice over: he cannot account either for the cooperation which is possible in a society without a Hobbesian Sovereign or for the dissension which is not only possible, but under some conditions more likely, in a society with one.

Chapter Four

THE COMMUNIST MANIFESTO

1

Marx's idea of the just society is no less distinctive than Plato's or Hobbes's. His definition of justice is a matter of dispute among the commentators, since his view that ideas are always relative to historical circumstance implies that bourgeois justice is peculiar to bourgeois society, and communist justice to communist society. But there is no doubt that the society which he wants to see is one in which private property has been abolished and resources are distributed from each according to ability to each according to need. That formulation of what was by then a cliché of French socialist thought comes from the *Critique of the Gotha Programme* of 1875, not from *The Communist Manifesto*. But in the *Manifesto*, it is clearly stated that the abolition of "modern bourgeois" private property (p. 538) will bring to an end the exploitation of the *Unterdrückte* by the *Unterdrücker*. Since the bourgeois state is no more than the executive committee (*Ausschuß*) of the bourgeois class (p. 528), once the proletariat has seized political power, the just society will come into being. Thereafter, "accumulated" (*aufgehäufte*) labour will only be a means to broaden, enrich, and advance the worker's "life process" (p. 540), and "the free development of each" will be "the condition for the free development of all" (p. 546).

There is an inescapable hint in this of recourse to preemptive definition reminiscent of Hobbes's in *Leviathan*. Any number of commentators, including the "Revisionists" of the 1890s, have remarked how little Marx ever said, either in the *Manifesto* or anywhere else, about the actual structure and operation of the communist society which would come into being in the aftermath of the revolutionary dictatorship of the proletariat. The *Manifesto* explicitly envisages that the proletariat will use its political *Herrschaft* to seize all capital from the bourgeoisie, to centralize all *Produktions-Instrumente* in the hands of the state, "which is to say of the proletariat organized as the ruling class," and to increase as rapidly as possible the "total sum of productive forces" (p. 545). But why should anyone believe that exploitation will thereafter be impossible? If the answer is that a class cannot exploit itself, what is to be said about rationally egoistic proletarians who continue to take advantage of one another where they can in the transactions in which they will continue to engage? When capital has been centralized and all private property surplus to immediate comsumption applied to public welfare, the allocation of resources will have to be regulated by those proletarians and their bourgeois allies who now make up the *Ausschuß* of the proletarian state, and the inequality of power between rulers and ruled will therefore be recreated in another form. Or if, alternatively, the proletarian *Ausschuß* disbands itself and resources centralized under its control are passed back to the workers who produced them, private property will re-emerge unless and until it is recentralized once again. There is no way out of this dilemma. No commentator, however sympathetic to Marx's vision of a society in which harmony and order are achieved and sustained by the expropriation of the expropriators, has ever been able to find one. On this issue, Marx cannot be acquitted of the charge that he is in his way as much of a utopian as the writers whom the *Manifesto* so vehemently denounces for their utopianism. A world of expanding productivity, uncontrolled freedom, and social equality is a sociological impossibility. His dilemma has been pointed out so many times in so many ways by so many commentators that little or nothing is left to be said except to ask why there is any need to repeat it yet again. The question to be asked is what it is that, despite this, could lead an eminent ex-Marxist Polish commentator still to say in the 1970s of the *Manifesto* that it is at the same time a "fundamental text of scientific socialism" and a "masterpiece of propagandist literature."[1]

---

[1] Leszek Kolakowski, *Main Currents of Marxism: Its Rise, Growth, and Dissolution* (Oxford, 1978), 1:228.

The answer given by Gareth Stedman Jones, the editor of the Penguin Classics edition of 2002, is that "The *Manifesto* will remain a classic, if only because of its brief but still quite unsurpassed depiction of modern capitalism," and that it "sketches a vision of reality that, at the start of a new millennium . . . looks as powerful and contemporary a picture of our own world as it might have appeared to those reading it in 1848."[2] But that can't be right. The vision of reality which the *Manifesto* presented to its readers in 1848 was real enough. There could be no mistaking the impact of capitalist industrialization on both Britain itself and the wider world—the disruption of traditional employment relations, the investment in increasingly advanced technology, the intensifying competition for profit between rival entrepreneurs, the forcible opening up of overseas markets, the improvements in both land-based and maritime transport, the agglomeration of factory workers in fast-expanding towns, the alternation of booms and slumps, and the concentration of ownership of larger units of production in fewer hands. But Marx and Engels saw, or thought that they saw, in all this a system in crisis in which the bourgeoisie that had brought it into being had thereby "produced its own grave-diggers" (p. 537). This, as everyone knows, turned out to be mistaken; and it was mistaken not just because

[2] Gareth Stedman Jones, introduction to *The Communist Manifesto*, by Karl Marx and Friedrich Engels (London, 2002), p. 5.

it was falsified by unpredictable contingent events but because the underlying analysis was flawed on four specific counts. Not merely did the proletarian revolution which Marx and Engels so confidently predicted in 1848 never happen, but it became less, not more, likely to happen for four by-now-unmistakable reasons which they had failed to see.

First, the wage labourers compelled to sell themselves as a commodity (p. 532) did not all sink deeper and deeper into "pauperism" (p. 537) as industrialization advanced. Economic historians have shown in exhaustive detail how changing methods of production and exchange affected different regions, different sectors of the economy, and different categories of wage workers in widely different ways. There were many workers who were indeed affected in the way that the *Manifesto* describes and for whom it meant loss of autonomy, devaluation of skill, recurrent unemployment, and a worsening of both living and working conditions. But there were many others who were not, or not to the degree that the *Manifesto* invites its readers to believe. However long it took for average real wages to rise and average hours of work to fall, that is what happened in the end; and at the same time that mechanization deskilled and impoverished some, it created a demand for new skills, new products, and new services which were provided by others. The average wage (*Durchschnittspreis der Lohnarbeit*) did not become fixed at nothing more than the minimum necessary to keep the worker in existence at all (p. 539).

Second, the lower middle classes (*kleinen Mittelstände*) neither "sank" into the proletariat (p. 533) nor were "hurled" (*hinabgeschleudert*) into it through their competition among themselves (p. 548). Not only did the traditional occupations so classified survive through the changes which followed from industrialization, but industrialization brought into being whole new categories of clerical and administrative occupations which came to form a growing rather than a diminishing proportion of the employed population.[3] It is true that sociologists continue to disagree about the number of classes into which a society such as Britain is divided. But although there is no one right answer, the roles constitutive of its economic institutions have always been too diverse for them to be placed on one or the other side of a single dividing line.

Third, the large factory (*große Fabrik*) into which modern industry is said to have transformed the "little workshop" (*kleine Werkstube*) of the "patriarchal master"

---

[3] Many commentators have pointed out how, later in his writings, Marx continued to assume a trichotomous structure of classes, sometimes (as the Polish sociologist Stanislaw Ossowski put it) in accordance with their different relationships to the means of production and sometimes in accordance with their relationships to the different means of production. *Class Structure in the Social Consciousness* (London, 1963), p. 81. But the *Manifesto* is categorical about the polarization of society, in the age of the bourgeoisie, into the "two great classes confronting each other directly" (p. 526).

(p. 532) was and remained less typical of industry as a whole than the *Manifesto* implies. Even in the textile industry where it first became the norm, the large factory took time to do so, and such diverse trades as, for example, building, clothing, coachbuilding, nail making, woodworking, printing, corn milling, food processing, laundering, carting, and stevedoring remained largely or wholly outside the factory system. By the time that industrialization and mechanization permeated the British economy to their furthest extent, conditions in the factories were no longer the same as they had been in Manchester in the 1840s when Engels was writing *The Condition of the Working Class in England*. Moreover, small establishments in the factory industries continued to outnumber large ones: a century after the publication of the *Manifesto*, three-quarters of the manufacturing establishments in Britain were still employing fewer than a hundred people, and even after establishments employing fewer than ten are excluded from the figures, they employed over a fifth of the total workforce. However dominant within certain sectors of British industry, the "industrial millionaires, the chiefs of whole industrial armies" (p. 527) whom Marx and Engels saw as taking the place of the industrial *Mittelstand* did not drive the role of small employer to extinction.

Fourth, the trade unions which were to bring about the "ever-widening unification (*Vereinigung*) of the workers" (p. 534) turned out to be much more concerned to resist

their bourgeois employers within the capitalist system
than to overturn the capitalist system by a proletarian revolution. The overriding aim of their leaders
was to defend the local and sectional interests of their
members. Some were more militant than others. But
even if they saw themselves as engaged in a collective
struggle against the employing class as such, their local
battles were never centralized in a national class war
of the kind that the *Manifesto* predicts. Had Marx and
Engels been there to see the mounting industrial un-
rest in Britain during the years before 1914, they would
no doubt have hailed it as a precursor of the downfall
of capitalism, just as they hailed the periodic financial
crises which they witnessed in their lifetimes. But the
"Triple Alliance" of transport workers, railwaymen, and
mineworkers in which some contemporary observers
saw the threat of an all-out general strike was not
formed to mount a proletarian revolution but only to
synchronize the timing of the expiry of existing collective agreements negotiated with the employers and
thereby bring pressure on Asquith's government to in-
tervene in the unions' favour. Nor did the Trade Union
Congress, despite its leaders' periodic anti-capitalist
rhetoric, ever have the power to coordinate, let alone
to override, the interests and rivalries of the separate
unions. "Syndicalism," as it was called, came closer to a
revolutionary programme of the kind of which Marx
and Engels would have approved. But in practice, the

conflict which it provoked was more between the rank and file and their official leaders than between the proletariat and the bourgeoisie.

All of this is by now thoroughly familiar to historians of all persuasions who have the benefit not only of hindsight but of a wealth of documentary and statistical evidence which researchers into the sociology of Victorian and Edwardian Britain have exploited to the full. It leaves present-day readers of the *Manifesto* as free as ever to share the moral indignation of its authors at the conditions which Marx and Engels described in 1848 and to feel a similar indignation at the exploitation of the *Unterdrückte* by the *Unterdrücker* which they can see all over the world around them in the present day. But that does nothing to remedy the weaknesses of arguments which, plausible as they may have seemed in 1848, have by now been invalidated beyond the possibility of recovery. Commentators sympathetic to Marx have sometimes argued that the reason why capitalism has survived is that the bourgeoisies of the capitalist societies have learned from Marx what they needed to do to avert the proletarian revolution which would otherwise have overwhelmed them. But the *Manifesto* did not consider this possibility at all. It predicted the inevitable self-destruction of capitalism, and its consequential replacement by a system in which private property, and therefore exploitation, would be abolished. No rereading can alter or circumvent that.

2

But if the *Manifesto* was wrong about the future, does it follow that it was wrong about the past? Not even the most vehement anti-Marxist can ignore the influence which Marx has had on the writing of history. However much he may have exaggerated the extent to which a society's ideological and political "superstructure" is determined by its economic "base," that does not warrant a dismissal out of hand of the *Manifesto*'s claims that changes in the mode of production cause a shift in political power corresponding to the economic advance of the now-dominant class, and that intellectual (*geistige*) production changes with material production (p. 543). But as an exercise in historical explanation, the *Manifesto* is flawed in two basic respects: first, its adherence to a Hegelian presupposition of teleology; and second, its oversimplification, deliberate as it may have been, of the transition which preceded the emergence of capitalism and the attendant evils which the proletarian revolution will put right.

Marx's early intellectual development is a fascinating story in itself. But despite his reaction against Hegel and then, in the 1840s, his mounting differences with so-called Young Hegelians, the commentators agree that he retained a conception of human history as leading to a predetermined outcome. In this, he was at one with any number of influential predecessors and contemporaries, Auguste Comte and Herbert Spencer among them. But

by the end of the twentieth century, it had become a
sociological commonplace that there is no master nar-
rative of human history or final goal towards which it is
leading but rather a continuous, path-dependent, open-
ended sequence of changes which are explicable only in
hindsight. There is a twofold irony in Marx's unreciprocated admiration for Darwin. He could not know that
whereas Darwin's theory of natural selection would be
triumphantly vindicated by twentieth-century advances
in population genetics and molecular biology, his own
theory of class conflict would be invalidated by the subsequent behaviour of proletariat and bourgeoisie alike. But
he also failed to realize that Darwin had not discovered a
lawlike sequence of biological evolution to which a supposedly lawlike sequence of modes of production would
be analogous, but that there are no laws of evolution at all.
The process of natural selection, like the processes of cultural and social selection which are continuous with it, is
one of open-ended variation, competition, and trade-off
which rules out any possibility of long-term prediction of
the future of either human society or the human species.

   Marx cannot be faulted for emphasizing the magnitude of the difference between the societies of Europe
as they had been before, and as they became in the
course of, the evolution out of feudalism into capitalism. But feudalism and capitalism are treacherous terms.
The suggestion that the citizens of the first towns, together with the small agricultural proprietors (*der kleine*

Bauernstand), were the "forerunners" (*Vorlaüfer*) of the "modern" bourgeoisie (p. 548) is uncontentious as far as it goes—if, that is, the explanandum is the acquisition through the market by private entrepreneurs of ownership and control of an increasing proportion of the means of production and their increasing employment of wage labour. But the institutional discontinuities which turned the medieval world into the modern world were a complex process driven by selective pressures in the modes of persuasion and coercion as well as production. In the history of England (to go no further afield), "feudalism" embraced a set of shifting practices, roles, and institutions which included conditional military tenure; vassalage; subinfeudation; ecclesiastical endowments; devolution of royal prerogatives; formal rules governing inheritance, succession, and marriage; manorial jurisdiction and customary rights; and codes of personal and family honour, as well as the whole spectrum of rights and duties bound up with tenure of land. The concept of capitalism, likewise, is more problematic than the *Manifesto* allows for. Marx was well versed in the law as well as the literature of ancient Roman society, which is, in the *Manifesto*, a pre-feudal and *a fortiori* "pre-capitalist" formation. But unless the existence of slavery—that is, ownership of persons— makes a society pre-capitalist by definition,[4] the Roman

---

[4] It is worth noting that Marx acknowledged explicitly the capitalist character of the antebellum American South and the capacity of slavery to gener-

economy was a system of practices and roles based on the private ownership of property in which impersonal transactions in cash were if anything more, not less, pervasive. It was, of course, a pre-industrial capitalism. But the *Manifesto*'s "*bare Zahlung*" (p. 528)—Carlyle's hated "cash nexus"—extended in Rome to the sale and purchase of votes, offices, judicial decisions, citizenship, gangs of armed men, applause by hired claques, and even the tickets which entitled the bearer to the corn dole, as well as of prostitutes, artworks, houses, businesses, and imported luxury goods. As the saying went, "Everything for Sale" (*Omnia Romae venalia*). There were wage workers, too, in the towns as well as on the land and down the mines. Increasing wealth became concentrated in fewer and fewer hands. There was a cultural prejudice among the elite against engaging directly in commerce, as there was in nineteenth-century England, but there were many entrepreneurs drawn from among former slaves and their descendants. Cash was often in short supply, but it was freely borrowed and lent at interest, and cash transactions were supplemented by the use of bills of exchange. Even if the story is a story about the societies of Europe only, to tell it as a unilinear progression from "ancient" slavery to "medieval" feudalism to "modern" capitalism is to oversimplify it far beyond what the evidence can bear.

---

ate capital accumulation: G. A. Cohen, *Karl Marx's Theory of History: A Defence* (Oxford, 1978), p. 185.

That is not to say that the forces and social relations of production have not been a strong and sometimes critical influence on the origin, course, and outcome of struggles between oppressors and oppressed. But it is to say that the *Manifesto* cannot be read as a reliable guide to the evolution of nineteenth-century European industrial, or industrializing, society out of the economic, ideological, and political institutions of the "ancient" and "feudal" modes which preceded it. Marx and Engels were not mistaken in seeing around them in 1848 a new and in many ways unprecedented system for the production, distribution, and exchange of material resources. But, as pointed out by one of the most perceptive of the commentators on Marxism, the *Manifesto* makes the mistake of taking the birth pangs of the new system to be death pangs.[5] Marx did, as is well known, subsequently modify his views about the preconditions for a successful proletarian revolution. But that was not so much a revision as a retraction of what the *Manifesto* had said.

It might at this point be objected that the *Manifesto* was only a preliminary statement of views that were to be formulated in mature form in the first volume of *Capital*, with its much wider range of descriptive and statistical evidence and its detailed exposition of Marx's labour theory of value. But the central proposition of

---

[5] George Lichtheim, *Marxism: An Historical and Critical Study* (London 1961), p. 58.

his theory of history, to which his much-criticised labour theory of value is only indirectly relevant, if at all, remained that of the opening sentence of part 1 ("*Bourgeois und Proletarier*") of the *Manifesto*: the history of all previous society is the history of *Klassenkampfe*. Conflict between economic classes defined by their relation to their society's mode of production is not only, for as long as the institution of private property is permitted to survive, what makes harmony and order impossible to achieve. It is also what has determined the relation between oppressors and oppressed ever since the human species emerged out of its primordial, pre-political condition into a world of cities, armies, temples, law courts, landed estates, foreign trade, and division and specialisation of labour. But is that correct?

The trouble begins, in the *Manifesto*, in the two paragraphs which follow the opening sentence of part 1. We are told that in the earlier epochs of history, although there was always a sometimes hidden and sometimes open *Kampf* between oppressors and oppressed, there was almost everywhere a much more complex gradation of ranks than the now-simplified confrontation between bourgeoisie and proletariat. In ancient Rome, there were patricians, knights, plebeians, and slaves; and in the Middle Ages, feudal lords, vassals, guild masters, journeymen, and serfs, with further gradations within each category. So were the conflicts between these all class conflicts? To that question, the answer has to be: some, but not all. In the Roman case, although class conflict was endemic in the relations between the owners of the means of production and the tenants, debt bondsmen, day labourers, craftsmen, domestic and agricultural or industrial slaves, and freed or servile supervisors, agents, administrators, and providers of services, it was not class conflict which brought about either the fall of the Roman Republic or the fall of the Roman Empire in the West. The Republic was brought down by struggles for control of the means of coercion between rival warlords whose soldiers gave their loyalty to them and not, as previously, to the Senate; and the Western Empire was weakened to the point of extinction by the inability of the rulers any longer to raise sufficient resources through taxation and booty to pay for its defence. There is no disagreement among historians of Rome about the oppression of the *Unterdrückte* by the *Unterdrücker* in both periods, as amply attested by documentary, epigraphic, and archaeological evidence. But the relations between them cannot all be assimilated to class conflict except by pre-emptive definition. This is what was done by G.E.M. de Ste. Croix in his formidably well-documented sociology of ancient Greece,[6] which also gives extensive coverage to ancient Rome. Written from an avowedly Marxist viewpoint, it expounds in detail the pervasive exploitation within

---

[6] G.E.M. de Ste. Croix, *The Class Struggle in the Ancient Greek World* (London, 1981).

Roman society of the propertyless by the propertied. But by assimilating to class struggle all forms of oppression of the weak by the strong, de Ste. Croix obscures the critical part played in the evolution of Roman society by both inter- and intra-systactic conflicts within the mode of coercion. The near-total breakdown of harmony and order in the late Republic and the chronic violence which accompanied it resulted in what the *Manifesto* calls a "revolutionary transformation (*Umgestaltung*) of the entire society" (p. 526) not in the sense of a seizure of power by a hitherto subordinate class, but of a violent redistribution of power within the ruling class which offered some increased opportunities of upward social mobility to ambitious provincials hitherto excluded from the Roman elite.

In the "feudal" Middle Ages, likewise, there can be no serious dispute about the oppression of the subordinate peasantry by their lords. The romantic vision of harmony and order in a world of chivalrous knights, pious clerics, and humble peasants looking to the knights for their protection and to the clerics for their salvation is as unreal as Plato's imagined world of wise Guardians, loyal Auxiliaries, and diligent Producers educated to be content in their appointed roles. But even if it is true that the bourgeoisie owes its political power to its ownership of the means of production, the *Feudalherren* (p. 527) owed their power to extract economic surpluses from the producers of them to their effective monopoly

of the means of coercion. The *Manifesto*'s mockery of
the "feudal socialism" of the French "Legitimists" and
"Young England," who, for all their anti-bourgeois rhetoric, in their political practice join the bourgeoisie in
imposing coercive regulations (*Gewaltmaßregeln*) on the
working class (p. 547) hits its target well. But the story
which the *Manifesto* tells of the transition from feudalism to capitalism is not a political story. It is a story in
which the "fetters" by which feudal property-relations
had constrained agricultural and manufacturing productivity were "sprung" (p. 531) and a revolutionary proletariat brought into existence by the workings of free
competition. For Marx and Engels, the political *Kon-
stitution* which went with it was its effect, not its cause.
The possibility that the power of the feudal lords was
broken by their surrender of the control of the means
of coercion to the central state and loss of the armed
retainers whom they supported with the surpluses ex-
tracted by force from their dependent cultivators is not
considered at all. The idea which to Hobbes was obvi-
ous, that the extent and degree of harmony or disorder
within a society depends more on its modes of coercion
and persuasion than its mode of production, is turned
on its head. The state can, of course, be controlled by
rulers who act in the interests of a dominant economic
class, just as it can be controlled by a clerical theocracy
with a monopoly of the means of persuasion. It can also
be controlled by an Athenian-type assembly which will

extract surpluses from richer citizens to the benefit of poorer ones. But Marx is committed *a priori* to denying an autonomous role in social evolution to political as opposed to economic relationships of dominance and subordination, from which it then follows that the achievement of harmony and order requires not the reform of the state but its abolition.

Lichtheim is also aware, as are other commentators likewise, that it is as difficult to fit the history of France into the *Manifesto*'s scheme as to fit that of England. The French Revolution is said to have "abolished feudal property in favour of bourgeois property" (p. 538). But if so, why has it not led on to a proletarian revolution? Until the last quarter of the twentieth century, Marxist historians continued to insist that since the French Revolution was a bourgeois revolution it was therefore an economic revolution. But it was not. It was a political one. The Revolutionaries did not overturn the existing system of property relations; industrialization and free competition within a rising entrepreneurial class was, if anything, retarded rather than advanced; the nobility, although they lost their seigneurial privileges and their monopoly of governmental roles, continued to participate, if they so chose, in agriculture, trade, and the gradual *pousée industrielle*; although the peasantry had played a decisive part in the overthrow of the monarchy, their economic position, including the traditional antagonism between town and countryside, was unchanged; when,

later in the nineteenth century, class conflict increasingly took the form of struggles over wages and conditions between worker (*ouvrier*) and boss (*patron*), it had
little or nothing to do with the events of 1789 to 1799.
Nor can the nineteenth-century changes of political regime and the violence which accompanied them be explained by pointing to a systemic contradiction between
the forces and social relations of production, any more
than the Revolution itself can be.

The further irony in this is that Marx's writings about
French politics, the effect of which on twentieth-century
readers Edmund Wilson was to describe as "electrical,"[7]
owe much of their force to a tacit disavowal of the
economic determinism of the *Manifesto*, particularly, as
Stedman Jones has pointed out,[8] in relation to the transition from Second Empire to Third Republic. Marx's
perceptive and often cynical insights into the motives
and strategies of the protagonists and his unmasking
of the economic interests at work behind the political
manoeuvrings retain all their rhetorical force. But the
constitutional history of nineteenth-century France and
the struggles of rival leaders and factions to establish
ideological legitimacy for one or another monarchical

---

[7] Edmund Wilson, *To the Finland Station: A Study in the Writing and Acting of
History* (New York, 1940), p. 203.

[8] Gareth Stedman Jones, "Marx's *Critique of Political Economy*: A Theory
of History or a Theory of Communism?" in *Marxist History-Writing for the
Twenty-First Century*, ed. Chris Wickham (London, 2007), p. 147.

or republican regime cannot be explained as a causal sequence in which the advance of capitalism compels the now-dominant bourgeoisie to drive an immiserated proletariat to revolution. The *Manifesto* chastises the "petty-bourgeois socialism" of Sismondi (p. 548) for failing to follow through the diagnosis of the contradictions of capitalist relations of production to a revolutionary conclusion. But France did not, and could not be made to, fit the *Manifesto*'s story of contradictions in the feudal mode of production leading inexorably to contradictions in the capitalist mode of production leading inexorably to proletarian revolution leading inexorably to a post-capitalist world of equality, plenty, and freedom.

3

In his preface to the German edition of 1890, Engels announced that although "few voices responded" in 1848 to the rallying cry "WORKING MEN OF ALL COUNTRIES, UNITE!" the "eternal union of the proletarians of all countries" which had been forged by the International Working Men's Association of 1864 "is still alive and lives stronger than ever." But the hope that a supra-national loyalty of workers to their class would be stronger than their intra-national loyalty to their state was an illusion which, as we now know, was to be brutally dispelled by the events of 1914. Not only Marxists but Liberals were to be startled by the bellicose patriotism of proletarians

of all countries who, far from signing up to a general
strike against the capitalist governments who were taking them into war, vociferously supported them. What
would have been the reaction of Marx and Engels if they
could have heard August Bebel as the avowedly Marxist
head of the German Socialists say that "the soil of Germany, the German fatherland, belongs to us the German
masses as much and more than to the others. If Russia, the champion of terror and barbarism, were to at-
tack Germany to break and destroy it . . . we are as much
concerned as those who stand at the head of Germany"[9]?

On this issue, both Plato and Hobbes were as realistic
as Marx and Engels were not. *Republic*'s Guardians and
Auxiliaries are to be trained as much to defend the ideal
society against its external enemies as to maintain internal harmony and order: as Plato's "Athenian Stranger"
puts it in the *Laws* (626a), "peace" is merely a state of
undeclared war between rival *poleis*. The Sovereign of
Leviathan likewise needs his untrammelled powers not
only to suppress sedition and prevent internal disorder
but to maintain his ability to protect the citizens of the
Commonwealth against the armies of hostile states. Pac-
ifism was as alien to Hobbes's thought as to Plato's. Both
agreed as unequivocally as each other with the principle that if you want peace you must prepare for war.

[9] Quoted by Michael Howard, *War and the Liberal Conscience* (London,
1977), p. 57.

Both would readily have grasped the idea of an internal revolution in which the poor rise up against their oppressors, drive them forcibly from power, and dispossess them of their property. But the idea that a simultaneous and coordinated uprising in every separate society and the redistribution of property which would follow it would usher in an era of universal peace would have struck them as ludicrous.

The reason for Marx's failure to acknowledge the power of nationalism was twofold. He underestimated, in a way that Max Weber never did, the strength of the autonomous political and ideological interests which sustain international anarchy and the extent to which industrialization and economic growth exacerbate international rivalry in some parts of the world at the same time that they further international cooperation in others. But he also held to an idealized picture of early human society which the researches of twentieth-century archaeologists, palaeoanthropologists, and evolutionary psychologists were to show to be untenable.[10] Marx's outrage at the inequitable distribution of resources between bourgeoisie and proletariat is fuelled in

---

[10]Engels, in a note which he added to the English edition of 1888, qualified the *Manifesto*'s "The history of all hitherto existing society is the history of class struggles" with a claim that since it was written research into the "prehistory of society" had revealed a world of "primitive Communist society" not yet differentiated into separate classes. But unless made so by pre-emptive definition, not all classless societies are communist any more than all communist societies are classless.

part by the abundance of the resources of which, with the help of new technology and new markets, the bourgeoisie takes and keeps for itself an indefensible share. He refuses to believe that the "Animals, Vegetables, and Minerals" of which Hobbes says in *Leviathan* that "God has freely layd them before us, in or near to the face of the Earth" (p. 170), must be shared as inequitably as they are. He believes that since private property, and the consequential exploitation by the propertied of the propertyless, is the cause of conflict between one society and another, its abolition must remove the occasion for conflict. There will no longer be any national bourgeoisies driven to go to war with one another in their relentless competition for profit, let alone feudal lords fighting for control of land and the serfs who work it or Roman generals embarking on wars of conquest in pursuit of booty and slaves. Universal revolution will usher in universal peace.

As Thrasymachus would say: *ō euēthestate*! How naive can you get?

Chapter Five

CONCLUSION

1

Although there is no universal standard against which the merits (or otherwise) of the conclusions advanced in these three famous books can be measured, nothing can turn an argument which fails on its own terms into a success. The arguments of Plato in *Republic*, Hobbes in *Leviathan*, and Marx and Engels in *The Communist Manifesto* which have been discussed in the previous chapters are strongly felt, artfully presented, and buttressed by carefully selected evidence. But they cannot be rescued from the objections which they invite. How is it, therefore, that all three books can continue, as they do, to be venerated as canonical texts in the European tradition of political thought and to be read and reread as they are by successive generations of students and commentators? The question which prompted the writing of this book still stands.

The answer to it must lie somewhere in the distinction drawn by the philosopher J. L. Austin between illocutionary and perlocutionary acts—between what someone does *in* saying what they say and what they do *by* saying it.[1] It is a distinction which has generated an extensive literature of its own, and I am not qualified to offer any opinion about the contribution that it may or may not have made to the solution of problems in the theory of meaning. But it directs the attention of readers of texts like these to the nature and consequences of the relation between the authors' intentions on the one hand and their own responses on the other in a way that suggests why bad arguments are not always as damaging to the reputations of their authors as it might seem natural to expect.

The extent of the perlocutionary effect of the three books is not in doubt. They have intrigued, stimulated, guided, inspired, and sometimes enraged innumerable readers and show every sign of continuing to do so. But they do it through locutions of widely different kinds and widely different illocutionary force. Any text which considers in any depth the causes of, and possible remedies for, conflict and disorder in human societies is likely not only to report how people behave and offer an explanation of why they behave as they do but also

[1] J. L. Austin, *How to Do Things with Words* (Oxford, 1962). It is perhaps worth noting that one example which Austin gives of an illocutionary act is cocking a snook (p. 118), which is what some readers may think I have been doing at Plato, Hobbes, and Marx. But let me re-emphasize that the illocutionary aim of this book is wholly serious, whatever may or may not be its perlocutionary effect.

to describe what it is like for the people themselves to behave as they do (and be treated by others as they are) and to assess their behaviour according to some evaluative standard. Plato, Hobbes, and Marx do all four of these things. But their reports are often questionable, their explanations often speculative, their descriptions often tendentious, and their evaluations often incoherent. The secret of their perlocutionary success has to be sought in the illocutionary force not of the different locutions contained in them when deconstructed one by one but of each text considered as a whole.

One possible conclusion to which this approach might be thought to lead is Burnyeat's. If, as he maintains, scope for diversity of interpretation is a virtue in itself, then all three texts can plausibly be claimed to exemplify it. *Republic* has variously been invoked in support of liberal idealism, conservative anti-modernism, utopian communism, national socialism, and republican egalitarianism.[2] *Leviathan* has been construed as an apology for tyranny by some, but Hobbes has been hailed as a "prehistoric Utilitarian" by others.[3] *The Communist Manifesto* was regarded in the decades after its republication in the German edition of 1872 as a by-then-outdated pioneering example of "scientific" socialism but was venerated after 1917 as a guide of immediate

[2] Melissa Lane, *Plato's Progeny: How Plato and Socrates Still Captivate the Modern Mind* (London, 2001), chap. 4.

[3] Deborah Baumgold, *Hobbes's Political Theory* (Cambridge, 1988), p. 56.

relevance and inspiration to the Communist parties of the world.[4] But is this diversity of readings really an argument in their favour? Clarity, admittedly, is not always an overriding imperative. Even if it is attainable in practice, it leaves room for all the ancillary analogies, similes, metaphors, and myths deliberately designed to entice the reader into the author's worldview. But to the extent that *Republic*, *Leviathan*, and *The Communist Manifesto* are seeking their readers' assent to their authors' conceptions of the good society, imprecision and ambiguity must be defects. How can well-educated philosopher-kings, wise and prudent sovereigns, or emancipated revolutionary proletarians follow the advice which will enable them to create and preserve harmonious and orderly societies if they are unclear in their own minds about what it is that they are being advised to do?

A different possible answer is that the illocutionary force of all three books is not so much political as religious. On this view, they are guides towards enlightened meditation on the meaning of human life and the nature of good and evil. Plato, after all, was enthusiastically assimilated by Philo, and after Philo by Plotinus, into the Judaeo-Christian tradition; Hobbes devoted much thought, and many pages of *Leviathan*, to the interpretation, or reinterpretation, of the Bible; and many

---

[4]Gareth Stedman Jones, introduction to *The Communist Manifesto*, by Karl Marx and Friedrich Engels (London, 2002), chap. 2 ("The Reception of the Manifesto").

of Marx's commentators have seen in him an Old Testament prophet combining eschatological prediction with moralistic denunciation in equal measure. Indeed, Marxism has itself been called a religion by a range of commentators including Schumpeter[5] as well as Popper and Kolakowski. But when Plato, in book 3 of *Republic*, has Socrates say to Adeimantus "Whither *logos* carries us like a wind, thither must we go" (394d), he is appealing not to revelation from on high but to reasoned argument. Hobbes, in *Leviathan*, although he approves of both invented and revealed religion to the extent that they make men "the more apt to Obedience, Lawes, Peace, Charity, and civill Society," sees the "Naturall seed of *Religion*" in "Opinion of Ghosts, Ignorance of second causes, Devotion towards what men fear, and Taking of things Causall for Prognostiques" (p. 79). In *The Communist Manifesto*, accusations against communism from a religious point of view are dismissed as undeserving of serious discussion (p. 543). It is one thing to say of Plato, Hobbes, and Marx that they have affinities with authors who address the same issues as they do from an avowedly religious perspective, but quite another to say that they are doing what Mohammed or Luther were doing—let alone Joseph Smith in founding Mormonism or Mary Baker Eddy in founding Christian Science.

[5] Joseph A. Schumpeter, *Capitalism, Socialism and Democracy* (London, 1943), p. 5.

Yet another possibility is that these books owe their lasting reputations to their literary rather than their academic merits. On this view, they should be read not in the way that avowedly scientific, historical, or metaphysical texts ask to be read but like novels whose fictional characters live in societies depicted in narratives which encompass sociological propositions about the forces at work in those societies, moral judgements about the virtues and vices of their representative denizens, and an implicit prefiguration of a new and better world. The literary merits of *Republic*, *Leviathan*, and *The Communist Manifesto* have long been recognized. *Republic* could even be said to be a novel of a kind, since its charming and vivid opening scene is a supposed meeting between Socrates and some of his friends which leads into a discursive conversation culminating in the myth of Er the Pamphylian—the myth that inspired the poem ("On Gorse") about the fate of the tyrant Ardiaios which was to be the last that the Nobel laureate George Seferis wrote. *Leviathan* is famous among people who have not read it, and never will, for the concluding paragraph of chapter 13 about the "state of Warre" and its ambience of "continuall feare, and danger of violent death; and the life of man, solitary, poore, nasty, brutish, and short" (p. 89). *The Communist Manifesto*'s account of the revolutionary historical part played by the bourgeoisie is made all the more memorable by the metaphors of the drowning of religious fervour and chivalrous enthusiasm in the "ice-cold water of egoistic calculation" (p. 528) and the sorcerer (*Hexenmeister*) who is "no longer able to control the infernal powers which he has conjured up" (p. 531). There can be no dispute that Plato, Hobbes, and Marx are all, among other things, gifted storytellers. But they are storytellers with a further purpose in mind. They are not setting themselves to do the same that George Eliot, say, in *Middlemarch*, or Thomas Mann in *The Magic Mountain* were setting themselves to do. They are using their literary gifts not merely to point a moral or adorn a tale but to lead their readers from stated premises to what they maintain to be valid conclusions. Similary, the commentators who successively analyse and reanalyse *Republic*, *Leviathan*, and *The Communist Manifesto* are not doing what a critic like Eric Auerbach, say, is doing in his *Mimesis*. They are analysts of the tradition not of Western literature but of Western political thought.

Perhaps, therefore, the solution is to be found by going back to Collingwood, rather than Burnyeat, and to the historians of ideas who insist on the need to interpret works like these from within their own temporal and local contexts. So stated, the injunction is one of which it might be said that all historians follow it as best they can without prompting. But to the contextualists, it is not enough merely to avoid anachronistic readings which credit authors with ideas that only their successors were in a position to formulate. It is necessary also to establish what they were querying, qualifying,

or denying in asserting what they did. All these are illocutionary acts which need to be deconstructed in
relation to the contemporaries and opponents whose
rival opinions are being queried, qualified, or denied.
In Plato's case, this is made difficult, although not impossible, by the fragmentary nature of the surviving
evidence for what his contemporaries and opponents
actually thought and taught. In Hobbes's case, enough
is known about his life and times for his reactions to
events and to the reaction of others to the same events
to be charted with considerable confidence. In the case
of Marx, the vehemence of his outspoken attacks on
those whom he saw as his enemies makes the task easier
still. But if their own arguments are persuasive only as
ad hominem rejoinders within conjunctions of unique
and increasingly remote historical circumstances, their
interest to us becomes correspondingly antiquarian. It
was undoubtedly, as a leading commentator on Hobbes
describes it, a "moment of great historical significance"
when, between his debate with Bramhall in the spring
of 1645 and his letter to Newcastle later that year, he
changed his mind about the definition of liberty.[6] That
change of mind has indeed had repercussions which
echo down to the present in arguments over "nega-
tive" versus "positive" liberty and the nature of political obligation. But the perlocutionary effect of *Republic,*

---

[6] Quentin Skinner, *Hobbes and Political Liberty* (Cambridge, 2008), p. 131.

Leviathan, and *The Communist Manifesto* in provoking and exacerbating controversy, and their consequential deployment as weapons in ideological warfare between rival political schools, are not in themselves enough to make them "great." It is not, after all, as if their effect has been to decide the outcome of the battle in favour of the side which has prayed them in aid. On the contrary: the polemics continue in part because so many of the arguments of *Republic*, *Leviathan*, and *The Communist Manifesto* have proved to be as inconclusive as they have. Whatever the historical significance of the three texts, both in their own time and since, there must be something else which gives them their enduring appeal to readers whose circumstances as are different as they are from those of Plato, or Hobbes, or Marx.

2

The contextualists are surely right to insist that there are no timeless concepts in the Western (or any other) tradition of political thought. The duty of the citizen to obey the rulers of a well-ordered society cannot, *pace* Plato's claims for reason, Hobbes's claims for science, and Marx's claims for dialectic, be demonstrated in the same way that, for example, already by Plato's time Greek mathematicians had demonstrated the irrationality of the square root of the number two. But concern about the potential for conflict and disorder which is inherent

in all known human societies *is* timeless. The particular forms which conflict and disorder take are, without question, historically contingent. Even when they
reappear in sometimes strikingly similar manifestations
at later times and in different places, the resemblance is
never more than partial. It can, perhaps, be argued that
there is a line of intellectual descent traceable back from
the eschatology of Marx through the French Revolutionaries and the Protestant millenarians to the Hebrew
prophets and before them to Zoroaster.[7] But the victory
of good over evil which, for Marx, emerges out of the
final showdown between bourgeoisie and proletariat is
something very different from the one which, for Zoroaster, emerges out of the final showdown between evil
as personified by Angra Mainyu and good as personified by Ahura Mazda. We don't need Collingwood to
remind us that "the thing has got *diablement changé en
route*." What is timeless is the abhorrence of conflict and
disorder as such.

If, accordingly, Plato, Hobbes, and Marx are read, in
Republic, Leviathan, and *The Communist Manifesto*, as
diagnosticians of the collective conflicts and disorders
which they observe and deplore in the world around
them, what kind of sociology are they doing? One possible answer is that they are doing *predictive* sociology:

---

[7] As is done by Norman Cohn, *Cosmos, Chaos, and the World to Come: The
Ancient Roots of Apocalyptic Faith* (New Haven, 1993).

they are telling their readers what will happen when the time is ripe and the potential rulers of the brave new world emerge from the wings onto centre stage to claim their inheritance. Another is that they are doing *normative* sociology: they are telling their readers how rulers and their subjects ought to behave once the brave new world has been brought into being. But these two interpretations are not the only possible ones; nor are they the most persuasive.

Of the three texts, *The Communist Manifesto* is the one whose illocutionary force can most plausibly be construed as predictive: the revolutionary transfer of power from bourgeoisie to proletariat is confidently asserted to be inevitable, and it will be assisted by the active efforts of those members of the bourgeoisie who acknowledge its inevitability. But how exactly will it come about? The answer given in the *Manifesto* is that it will come about through a process of dissolution (*Verlösungsprozess*) which divides the ruling class against itself (p. 535) as well as by the forecast unification of the workers. But since these two things are precisely what *didn't* happen in England, any more than did the extinction of the lower middle class and the small employer, it can hardly be success in foretelling the future that sustains the *Manifesto*'s iconic status. Still less could this be claimed for either *Republic* or *Leviathan*. Both Plato and Hobbes wish to persuade their readers that their brave new worlds are not, despite the acknowledged obstacles in the way, wholly impossible of realization. In book 6 of *Republic*, Socrates undertakes to demonstrate, difficult though he knows it to be, how a *polis* could practise philosophy without being destroyed by it (497d), and Hobbes, at the end of *Leviathan*, reaffirms his belief that "Education, and Discipline" can reconcile in "Civill Amity" those engaged in a "perpetuall contention for Honor, Riches, and Authority" (p. 483). But neither goes so far as to say that this happy state of affairs is inevitable.

The illocutionary force of all three texts is normative to the extent that Plato, Hobbes, and Marx are explicit in their disapprobation of the kinds of people whose behaviour gives rise to the conflict and disorder which they deplore. Readers of *Republic* are left in no doubt about what Plato thinks of power-mad tyrants, irresponsible demagogues, greedy oligarchs, and farmers, artisans, and businessmen with pretentions above their station. Readers of *Leviathan* are left in no doubt about what Hobbes thinks of disobedient subjects, seditious clerics, self-seeking counsellors, and hot-headed malcontents who conspire against their rulers. Readers of *The Communist Manifesto* are left in no doubt about what Marx and Engels think of cold-hearted capitalist employers, hypocritical bourgeois ideologues, reactionary pseudo-socialists, and exploitative landlords and shopkeepers. But these denunciations, eloquent and forceful though they are, cannot by themselves account for the lasting reputation of works in which they are subordinated to a larger aim. Individual misbehaviour, reprehensible as it may be, is a symptom of deeper, systemic failure. Plato's irresponsible demagogues, Hobbes's disobedient subjects, and Marx's cold-hearted capitalists are all acting under influences which they cannot understand, let alone control, without the help and guidance which Plato, Hobbes, and Marx are there to give them.

If there is a single genre to which the three texts can all be assigned, it is that of *optative* sociology. Their illocutionary mode is neither that of "This is what is going to come about" nor that of "This is what ought to come about" but that of "If only this *were* to come about, how much better a place the world would be!" They are masterpieces of anger transmuted into hope. Plato longs for a world in which wise and good rulers have educated the ruled to be wise and good too. Hobbes longs for a world in which strong and sensible rulers have deterred the ruled from turbulence and treason. Marx longs for a world in which the oppression of the ruled by their rulers has been done away with by the abolition of the institution that causes it. Surely, all three want to say to their readers, things don't have to go on being as bad as they are—do they?

Optative sociology is not to be confused with utopian sociology. Neither Plato nor Hobbes nor Marx envisage a world in which nobody is lazy or dishonest, nobody gets angry, nobody inflicts harm on anybody else, nobody is greedy for riches or prestige or political power, and nobody prefers winning to losing. All three take men as they are (their views about women being a separate matter about which, despite the role assigned by Plato to female Guardians, all three say much too little). But they know that people would be other than they are if they had been brought up in a different way and led their lives in a different cultural and social environment. To the extent that upbringing and environment can be changed, it must be possible so to reform existing institutions as to make human societies more harmonious and orderly than they presently are. Not all human beings behave as badly as the bad ones do. Not all societies are riven by conflict to the same degree. Not every other-regarding act is motivated by fear of reprisal or hope of reward. Cooperative strategies can under some conditions be evolutionarily stable. Some mutations of economic, ideological, and political practices can benefit ruled and rulers alike. Cannot human beings, therefore, be brought to live in peace with one another? Does Thrasymachus have to be right?

However weak the arguments in *Republic*, Plato was entitled to believe that human reason is capable at arriving at an intellectual understanding of truths which can be applied to the enhancement of human well-being. However weak the arguments in *Leviathan*, Hobbes was entitled to believe that there is in human psychology an innate disposition not only to fear death but to accept that protection against anarchy, violence, and dispossession implies an obligation of some kind to the protector. However weak the arguments in *The Communist Manifesto*, Marx was entitled to believe that it is within the scope of human intelligence and skill to moderate the extreme inequalities which arise through unregulated competition for material resources. The ten-point wish list of practical measures at the end of the chapter in the *Manifesto* on "Proletarians and Communists" is anything but unrealistic: much of it, including progressive income tax and centralization of credit in national state-controlled banks, has happened already, as commentators of all political persuasions have seen for themselves.

No reading of these texts can be definitive, and I claim for my own only that it suggests an answer to the question of my own with which I set out. Perhaps it is only because I reread them, as I did, in sequence after half a century of reflection of my own about the workings of human societies of different kinds that they seem to me to share the same overriding preoccupation with the same timeless concern about how harmony and order in human societies are to be created and sustained. But they fell naturally into place as successive attempts to respond, in their different ways, to Thrasymachus's challenge. Thrasymachus would be entitled to say that two and a half millennia of human history have shown how right he was to upbraid Socrates for his naivety. But he would not be entitled to say that his view of how people behave towards one another is right everywhere, in every respect, all the time.

3

I opened this book with an anecdotal reminiscence of a conversation with an eminent philosopher, and I end it with another one.

The philosopher this time is Herbert Hart, who chaired a seminar in Oxford about John Rawls's *A Theory of Justice* shortly after its publication in 1971. I was there at my own invitation because I had been the then-anonymous front-page reviewer of Rawls's book for the *Times Literary Supplement*. In my review, I predicted—as it turned out, correctly—that *A Theory of Justice* would be the most influential contribution to political philosophy in the Western liberal tradition since Mill and Sidgwick. But I also suggested, as many better-qualified commentators were to do thereafter, that Rawls's idea of an "original position," in which the parties to a primordial contract agree from behind a "veil of ignorance" on the principles which are to guide the distribution of resources in the society in which they will find themselves, doesn't actually work. It looks like another example of bad arguments and a great book. Not only is Rawls's theory sociologically uninformed—there is nothing in it of comparative history or ethnography—but a hypothetical payoff matrix can easily be constructed such that no player in the original position could seriously be expected to opt for the strategy dictated by one of the principles to which Rawls supposes that every rational person would subscribe.

At the seminar, I was too much in awe of Hart to take any part in the discussion. But in conversation after it, he surprised me by saying that he thought the second half of the book much better than the first. He meant by this not simply that the arguments of the first part are not strong enough to sustain the conclusions which Rawls seeks to draw from them. He also meant that the second part puts before the reader a deeply considered, carefully elaborated, and intuitively appealing depiction of what a society would be like which conformed to Rawls's idea of justice. Rawls has been criticized, and sometimes vehemently so, for having too obviously in mind an idealized picture of his own society, which as a young man he had fought to defend against fascism in World War II. But I still think that Hart was right. Whether *A Theory of Justice* will find a place on a ca-nonical reading list for future generations of students of political thought alongside *Republic*, *Leviathan*, and *The Communist Manifesto*, I do not know. But if it does, it will be because it, like they, transcends its context to address perennial concerns shared by anyone who regrets that harmony and order should be so dismayingly difficult for human beings living together in their various societ-ies to achieve.